Stand Out

5

Reading & Writing Challenge

Staci Johnson • Rob Jenkins

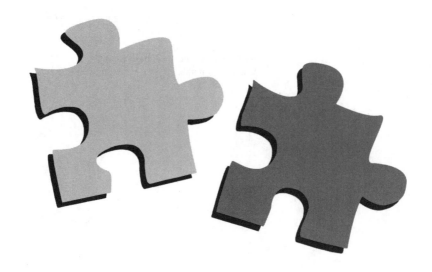

HEINLE
CENGAGE Learning™

Australia • Canada • Mexico • Singapore • Spain • United Kingdom • United States

Stand Out 5 Reading & Writing Challenge
Staci Johnson and Rob Jenkins

Publisher: Sherrise Roehr

Acquisitions Editor: Tom Jefferies

Assistant Development Editor: Cécile Engeln

Director of Content and Media Production:
 Michael Burggren

Product Marketing Manager: Katie Kelley

Sr. Content Project Manager:
 Maryellen E. Killeen

Sr. Print Buyer: Mary Beth Hennebury

Cover / Text Designer: Studio Montage

Compositor: Parkwood Composition
 Service, Inc.

ISBN 10: 1-4240-6899-1
ISBN 13: 978-1-4240-6899-9

Heinle
20 Channel Center Street
Boston, MA 02210
USA

Cengage Learning is a leading provider of customized learning solutions with office locations around the globe, including Singapore, the United Kingdom, Australia, Mexico, Brazil and Japan. Locate our local office at:
international.cengage.com/region

Cengage Learning products are represented in Canada
by Nelson Education, Ltd.

Visit Heinle online at **elt.heinle.com**
Visit our corporate website at **cengage.com**

Printed in the United States of America.
2 3 4 5 6 7 8 9 10 11

CONTENTS

TO THE TEACHER

About *Stand Out: Standards-Based Learning*

The *Stand Out* series includes a six-level basal series for English language learners designed to facilitate active learning, while challenging students to build a nurturing and effective learning community.

About *Stand Out Reading & Writing Challenge*

Stand Out Reading & Writing Challenge was written to give students additional practice in vocabulary, reading, and writing, while focusing students' attention on life-skill content.
Stand Out Reading & Writing Challenge is aligned with the basal series and is divided into eight distinct units, mirroring competency areas most useful to newcomers. These areas are outlined in CASAS assessment programs and different state modal standards for adults.
No prior content knowledge is required to use *Stand Out Reading & Writing Challenge.* However, students will need the skill background necessary for their particular level. The books can be used as a supplemental component to *Stand Out* or as a stand-alone text.

Philosophy of *Stand Out Reading & Writing Challenge*

Stand Out Reading & Writing Challenge is intended for English language learners who need more practice with vocabulary, reading, and writing than they are given in most basal texts. Each unit takes students from a life-skill activity to vocabulary and reading practice and eventually to a finished piece of writing with the philosophy that students learn best when actively engaged in activities that relate to their personal lives and move from what they already know to new information.

Organization of *Stand Out Reading & Writing Challenge*

Stand Out Reading & Writing Challenge challenges students to develop their vocabulary, reading, and writing skills through eight unique units. Each unit includes a mix of activity types and caters to students with different learning styles.

▶ **Life-Skill Activity** Each unit opens with a life-skill activity designed to activate students' prior knowledge about the topic and prepare them for the following activities.

▶ **Vocabulary** Students are introduced to vocabulary that they need to better understand the reading. They will go through a series of activities designed to make them more familiar with the vocabulary and how it will be used. The lower levels use a variety of pictures to demonstrate much of the vocabulary. The higher levels introduce dictionary skills to help students become more independent learners.

▶ **Life-Skill Readings** Students will prepare for the reading by assessing their own knowledge and by making predictions about what they will read. Following the reading, they will do a variety of comprehension activities as well as expansion activities designed to help them relate the reading to their own lives.

TEXT CREDITS

Unit 1

"Realize Your Dreams"
From the book *Chicken Soup to Inspire a Woman's Soul* by Jack Canfield, Mark Victor Hansen, and Stephanie Marston. Copyright 2004 by Chicken Soup for the Soul Publishing, LLC. Published by Health Communications, Inc. Chicken Soup for the Soul is a registered trademark of Chicken Soup for the Soul Publishing, LLC. Reprinted by permission. All rights reserved.

Unit 2

From Lawrence J. Gitman/Michael D. Joehnk. *Personal Financial Planning*, 11E. © 2008 South-Western, a part of Cengage Learning, Inc. Reproduced by permission. www.cengage.com/permissions

Unit 3

"What's Next in Auto Safey"
Copyright 2007 by Consumers Union of U.S., Inc. Yonkers, NY 10703-1057, a nonprofit organization. Reprinted with permission from the April 2007 issue of CONSUMER REPORTS® for education purposes only. No commercial use or reproduction permitted. www.ConsumerReports.org

Unit 5

From GARMAN. *Personal Finance*, 9E. © 2008 South-Western, a part of Cengage Learning, Inc. Reproduced by permission. www.cengage.com/permissions

Unit 6

"Going local" by Twilight Greenaway
Reprinted with permission. This article originally appeared at culinate.org on January 29, 2007.

Unit 7

"How Hard Could It Be?: Thanks or No Thanks" by Joel Spolsky
Reprinted with permission from *Inc. Magazine*, January 2009.

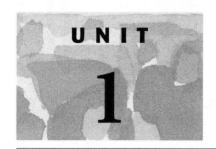

UNIT 1

Balancing Your Life

▶ GETTING READY

A Look at the form that Margie filled out. Discuss the questions below.

What I do now	What I want to do	Impossible dream
Work as a counselor at a high school	Go to college and get a degree in marketing	Learn how to play a drum and join a drumming group

1. What is Margie's current job?
2. What degree does she want to get?
3. What can she do with a marketing degree?
4. What is her impossible dream?
5. Why do you think she believes this is impossible?

B Complete the form below about yourself.

What I do now	What I want to do	Impossible dream

C Take out a piece of paper and describe your impossible dream. Why is it impossible?

▶ VOCABULARY CHALLENGE

A Look at the words. Check (✔) the words that you know.

☐ vibrant   ☐ courage   ☐ resign   ☐ vision   ☐ discomfort

☐ embark   ☐ expertise   ☐ fulfilling   ☐ generate   ☐ intriguing

☐ journal   ☐ mainstream   ☐ manifest   ☐ meditate   ☐ visualize

B Read the sentences. Then write the underlined word next to the correct definition.

1. One of the classes sounded <u>intriguing</u>, so I signed up for it.
2. Our imaginations are real and <u>vibrant</u>, and can be used to fill our lives with such joy.
3. I spent my days learning that teaching drumming was not only fairly easy for me but also joyful and <u>fulfilling</u>.
4. The student musicians were mostly younger, offbeat, not your <u>mainstream</u> types.

   a. _____ satisfying

   b. _____ typical, normal, conventional

   c. _____ interesting

   d. _____ full of life, energy, and enthusiasm

C Answer the questions about yourself.

1. José is a mechanic. His expertise is in fixing cars. What do you have expertise in?

     _____

2. It causes me discomfort to talk about money. What causes you discomfort?

     _____

3. I have a journal that I write in every night. I like to write about what I did during the day and how it made me feel. If you had a journal, what would you write about?

     _____

D It takes courage to do something new in your life. Describe a time when you had courage.

     _____

     _____

     _____

E Complete the sentences below. Change the form of the verb if necessary.

Verb	Definition	Example sentence
embark	to begin doing something new, difficult, or exciting	I named my business "Heartbeats," because I loved with all my heart the journey I was embarking on.
manifest	when a particular quality or feeling becomes visible	The idea of becoming a drummer began to manifest itself in my life.
generate	to cause something to begin and develop	I loved the heart-pounding rhythms that were being generated.
meditate	to remain in a silent and calm state for some time	I walked on the beach, meditated, read, and shopped at the local craft shops.
visualize	to imagine what something is like by forming a mental picture	We were told to stick with our original idea, and start journaling, visualizing, and acting like we had already reached our goal.
resign	to formally announce that you are leaving a position	At the age of forty-eight, I resigned from nineteen years at the high school.

1. In order to relax in the mornings before I leave for work, I like to _____.

2. When he decided to become a photographer, he started _____ himself taking photographs every day.

3. Our family _____ on a new journey by selling our house and buying a boat to sail around the world.

4. Once the idea of starting her own business began to _____

   itself, she was ready to _____ from her job.

5. They started _____ ideas of how to raise enough money to start their non-profit organization.

▶ **ACADEMIC WORD LIST**

F The Academic Word List is a list of words that are most commonly found in academic reading. Which ones do you know?

☐ journal   ☐ vision   ☐ community   ☐ generated   ☐ purchasing

☐ coordinator   ☐ visualizing   ☐ consisted   ☐ energy   ☐ equipment

☐ role   ☐ goal   ☐ found   ☐ expertise   ☐ license

☐ grade   ☐ couple   ☐ despite   ☐ instruct   ☐ create

Look at the following expressions. Then complete the sentences below with the correct expression.

Expression	Definition
stirrings of discontent	the beginning feelings of not being satisfied
doors will start opening	opportunities will present themselves
hairs stand up on my arms	chills; something that greatly affects you
stick it out	not leaving or giving up
out of reach	not possible to have or get
turning point	a time at which an important change takes place which affects the future

1. Her college classes were so difficult that she feared she might fail them. But, she decided to _____.

2. He began to feel the _____ at his job, as if there were something more out there for him.

3. They really wanted to sell their house and move to another country but they felt that this dream was _____.

4. As soon as she graduates, she knows that _____.

5. The sisters knew that getting a scholarship to the school of their choice would be a _____ in their lives.

6. The music was so beautiful that it made the _____.

H **Discuss the following questions with a small group.**

1. Talk about a situation in which you stuck it out.
2. Is there a goal you have that you think is out of reach?
3. Has there ever been a turning point in your life?
4. What makes the hair stand up on your arms?
5. Has something ever happened where doors started opening for you?

► DICTIONARY WORK

I In order to be able to use a dictionary, it is important to understand all the components of a dictionary entry. Look at the entry below.

dictionary entry | pronunciation | part of speech

vision /vɪ3°n / (visions) 1 n-count Your **vision** of a future situation or society is what you imagine or hope it would be like if things were very different from the way they are now. *I have a vision of myself moving to another country.* 2 n-non-count Your **vision** is your ability to see clearly with your eyes. *The doctor said I have excellent vision.* 3 n-non-count Your **vision** is everything you can see from a particular place or position. *The trees blocked my vision and I didn't see the deer in the road.*

definition →

example sentence

J Answer the questions.

1. How many definitions are there for *vision*? _____

2. What part of speech are all the definitions? _____

3. What is the difference between a count and non-count noun? _____

    _____

4. Write your own example sentences, one for each of the three definitions.

    1. _____

    2. _____

    3. _____

K The definition above was taken from the *Collins Cobuild Intermediate Dictionary of American English.* Look up the same word in your dictionary. How is it the same? How is it different? Share your ideas with a partner.

L Choose three of the new vocabulary words you have learned in this unit that you would like to know more about. Look up each word in your dictionary. Write their complete dictionary entries on a separate piece of paper. Write an example sentence for each word below.

    1. _____

    2. _____

    3. _____

▶ PRE-READING

A **Read the following quote. What do you think it means?**

> *"Each day comes bearing its own gifts. Untie the ribbons."*

B **Answer the following questions about yourself.**

1. If you could do anything in the world (that you aren't doing now) what would you do?

   _____

   _____

2. Have you ever tried to do something that you didn't think you could do? If so, what was it? Were you successful?

   _____

   _____

C **Share your answers with a partner.**

D **Look at the picture below. Who do you think this is? What is she doing? What do you think the story will be about?**

Read the story.

Realize Your Dreams

BY MARGIE PASERO

Each day comes bearing its own gifts. Untie the ribbons. ~Ruth Ann Schabacker

I had been working at a job I loved, an attendance coordinator at a high school, for eighteen years when I began to feel the stirrings of discontent. I had always been in a disciplinarian[1] role and it was becoming uncomfortable. I felt as though I wasn't being true to myself in this role. I was ten years away from retirement and had decided to stick it out when the school district sent me to a weekend workshop. One of the classes, "Realizing Your Dreams," sounded intriguing, so I signed up for it.

After being introduced to the presenter, we were asked to close our eyes and think as far back as we could remember. What was it we loved to do most in the world? What had excited us and made us feel alive? We were to allow whatever came to our minds to be there, no matter how bizarre[2] it might seem. The word "rhythm" came to my mind. I had loved it as a youngster. I had played the clarinet[3] since third grade but had always wanted to be the kid behind the drums. However, during the fifties, girls usually played the flute,[4] clarinet or piano. In high school, my dream had been to be in a rock band, but after years of playing the clarinet, learning to play the drums and joining a rock band seemed out of reach.

The presenter then gave us several exercises to take home. He said if we did the exercises religiously our "vision" would crystallize[5] and manifest itself in our lives. At this point, I was thinking that drumming at the age of forty-five was probably a bit "out there,[6]" and maybe I should come up with something more suited to[7] my age group. However, we were told to stick with our original idea, and start journaling, visualizing and acting like we had already reached our goal. It didn't matter, he said, that we had no idea at this moment exactly what the goal was . . . just do the exercises. He also said that doors would start opening in our lives, and we would need to recognize them as opportunities and walk through them—even if they felt uncomfortable at the time.

I don't know how many people in the class actually went home, did the exercises and realized a dream, but I decided I would try it. I bought myself a spiral notebook, and every morning I sat quietly and wrote a full page of "I am a drummer . . . I am a drummer . . . I am a drummer." I said this mantra[8] to myself over and over during the day, and started to imagine myself drumming. All this seemed weird at the beginning, but it actually started to feel exciting and "right" after a couple of weeks.

After about two weeks of journaling and visualizing, my sister called to ask me if I knew about the large African drumming community in Seattle. I hadn't known about this, but I imagined that the community consisted of either Africans, which I am not, or hippies, which I am no longer. I did recognize this as a door opening, however, and decided to take a drumming class. The first

---

[1] **disciplinarian** – person who makes and/or enforces rules
[2] **bizarre** – very odd or strange
[3] **clarinet** – a wind instrument with a single reed in its mouthpiece.
[4] **flute** – a musical instrument of the woodwind family. You play it blowing over a hole near one end while holding it sideways to your mouth.
[5] **crystallize** – when an opinion or idea becomes fixed and definite in your mind
[6] **out there** – crazy, strange
[7] **suited to** – appropriate for
[8] **mantra** – a repeated word or phrase

six months found me in a group of people I judged to be very different from me. They were mostly younger, off-beat,[9] not your mainstream types. Despite my discomfort, I found I loved the heart-pounding rhythms[10] that were being generated. Soon after, I bought my first drum—it called to me; it had an energy that was powerful, yet simple and beautiful.

Several months later, I was at Seattle's Folklife Festival where I saw a group of children performing on African drums. It made the hairs stand up on my arms and brought tears to my eyes . . . this powerful sound coming from children! That was the crystallizing moment for me. I realized then and there that I wanted to take my educational experience and my love of drumming and teach children. I gathered my courage and spoke to the director, Kip, after the performance. He was excited to share his expertise and invited me to come to Port Townsend in the summer to help him teach a summer drumming camp. In August 1999, I boarded the Seattle to Port Townsend ferry alone for my adventurous weekend. I pampered[11] myself by staying in an old Victorian hotel. I spent my days learning that teaching drumming was not only fairly easy for me but also joyful and fulfilling. Kip was more than willing to let me instruct and give me information on starting my own business, purchasing drums and equipment, and lining up jobs. In the evenings, I walked on the beach, meditated, read, took in a movie and shopped at the local craft shops. I will always remember that weekend as a turning point in my life, spiritually as well as occupationally.

Back at home, I started fine-tuning[12] my journaling: "I am a drumming teacher . . . I am a drumming teacher . . . I am a drumming teacher." My husband started introducing me as a drumming teacher, even though I still worked at the high school and only had one drum. I continued taking lessons and performing with my class; I started feeling a part of the Seattle drumming community. At this point, I knew I had to take this "game" I was playing to a different level, or it would always be just a game.

Just before the turn of the new millennium,[13] at the age of forty-eight, I resigned from nineteen years at the high school, bought ten drums and a basketful of small percussion instruments, printed business cards, got a business license, and made flyers describing my goals, spiritual intentions and drumming experience. I started calling parks departments, schools, Boys and Girls Clubs and YMCAs. I named my business "Heartbeats," because I loved with all my heart the journey I was embarking on. I was terrified but I did it. Now, four years later, I have a wonderful business where teaching drumming allows me to play instead of work.

In addition to teaching drumming, I also felt a great need to be a performer in a women's drumming group. I wanted our songs to be original compositions[14] with a spirit-filled agenda. I wanted to be part of a group that played not only drums, but also other instruments to give it an unusual and interesting flavor.[15] I started journaling these intentions and am now a member of OmBili Afro-Cuban Tribal Jazz all-women performing troupe.

I believe that we all can create whatever is in our hearts. We just need to visualize it, journal it, and feel what it is like to have accomplished it. It works for anything in life. Our imaginations are real and vibrant, and can be used to fill our lives with such joy.

---

[9] **off-beat** – different
[10] **heart-pounding rhythms** – a series of sounds that make one's heart beat faster
[11] **pamper** – take care of someone, do something nice for someone
[12] **fine-tuning** – making better
[13] **millennium** – one thousand years
[14] **compositions** – pieces of written music
[15] **flavor** – distinctive quality

► SKIMMING FOR DETAILS

F **Write *True* or *False* on the line. Rewrite the false statements and make them true.**

                   an attendance coordinator
EXAMPLE: Margie was ~~a principal~~ at a high school.   ___false___

1. Margie played the drums when she was a child.   _____

2. Margie's sister told her about an African drumming community
   in Seattle.   _____

3. In June of 1999, she went to help teach a drumming camp.   _____

4. Margie's husband started introducing her as a disciplinarian.   _____

5. Margie resigned from her job at the high school when she was 38.   _____

6. She had worked there for 19 years.   _____

7. Margie named her business Heartbeats.   _____

8. Besides teaching drumming, Margie is also a secretary.   _____

► SEQUENCING

G **Number the events below (1-12) in the order they occurred in the story.**

_____ Kip invited me to come to Port Townsend in the summer to help him teach a
summer drumming camp.

_____ The school district sent me to a weekend workshop where I signed up for a class
called, "Realizing Your Dreams."

_____ Several months later, I was at Seattle's Folklife Festival where I saw a group of
children performing on African drums.

_____ I bought ten drums and a basketful of small percussion instruments, printed
business cards, got a business license, and made flyers.

_____ The presenter told us to start journaling, visualizing, and acting like we had
already reached our goal.

_____ I resigned from the high school.

_____ I bought myself a spiral notebook, and every morning I sat quietly and wrote a
full page of "I am a drummer . . . I am a drummer . . . I am a drummer."

_____ I became a member of OmBili Afro-Cuban Tribal Jazz all-women performing
troupe.

_____ I decided to take a drumming class.

_____ I had been working at a job I loved, an attendance coordinator at a high school,
for eighteen years when I began to feel the stirrings of discontent.

_____ After about two weeks of journaling and visualizing, my sister called to ask me if
I knew about the large African drumming community in Seattle.

_____ I continued taking drumming lessons and performing with my class.

Circle the best answer.

1. Why was Margie feeling discontent at her job?
   a. She attended a workshop about realizing dreams.
   b. She felt like she wasn't meant to be a disciplinarian.
   c. She wanted to become a drummer.
   d. Retirement was too far away.

2. Why did Margie think drumming was out of her reach?
   a. She already had a job.
   b. She was too old to become a drummer.
   c. She didn't know how to play the drums.
   d. She had played the clarinet as a child.

3. What helped open the door for Margie to take a drumming class?
   a. Her friend Kip invited her to teach at a summer camp.
   b. The school district sent her to a workshop.
   c. She bought a notebook and wrote down her mantra.
   d. Her sister told her about the large African drumming community in Seattle.

4. Where was Margie when she realized that she wanted to teach children?
   a. Seattle's Folklife Festival
   b. Port Townsend
   c. the old Victorian hotel
   d. her school

5. What were Margie's two mantras?
   a. "I am a drummer" and "I can play the drums"
   b. "I am a performer" and "I play the drums"
   c. "I am a drummer" and "I am a drumming teacher"
   d. "I am a drumming teacher" and "I teach drumming to children"

6. What did Margie NOT do to get her business started?
   a. She bought drums and percussion instruments.
   b. She pampered herself.
   c. She got a business license.
   d. She contacted local organizations to find students.

7. What did Margie decide she wanted to do in addition to being a drumming teacher?
   a. She wanted to be a performer in a women's drumming group.
   b. She wanted to compose music.
   c. She wanted to learn to play another instrument.
   d. She wanted to resign from her job.

I **Answer the questions in your own words.**

    1. What helped Margie realize that she wanted to become a drummer? _____

            _____

    2. What word came to her mind when she thought about what made her feel excited

        and alive? _____

    3. What was her vision? _____

            _____

    4. In addition to writing her mantra, what else did Margie do to make the idea of

        becoming a drummer more real to her? _____

            _____

    5. Why did Margie think she wouldn't fit in with the African drumming community?

            _____

    6. What was so special about the first drum she bought? _____

            _____

    7. What made her decide that she wanted to teach children? _____

            _____

    8. What was the turning point in her life? _____

            _____

    9. What made her feel a part of the Seattle drumming community? _____

            _____

  10. Reread and summarize the last paragraph of the reading.

            _____

            _____

            _____

            _____

▶ **EXTENSION**

J **Find out more about Margie at http://www.learningmusician.com/mdrummerp**

▶ WRITING CHALLENGE: Narratives

A A narrative is a piece of writing that tells a story. Why is "Realizing Your Dreams" considered a narrative? What story does it tell?

▶ BRAINSTORM: Choosing a Topic

B Answer the following questions about yourself. Think carefully about your answers before you write.

1. What do you love to do most in the world?

   _____

2. What excites you and makes you feel alive?

   _____

   _____

3. Based on your two answers from above, what would be a vision of you doing what you loved? _____

   _____

4. Write a mantra for yourself. _____

   _____

▶ CHOOSE A TOPIC

C You will be writing your own story. Choose one of the following topics for your narrative. Circle the topic you choose.

1. Tell the story of how you made your impossible dream come true.
2. Tell the story of a friend who made his or her impossible dream come true.
3. Imagine that your impossible dream has become a reality. Tell the story.

▶ BRAINSTORM: Ideas for Your Story

D **Look back at the Sequence of Events you numbered in Exercise G on page 9. Write the sequence of events for your narrative below.**

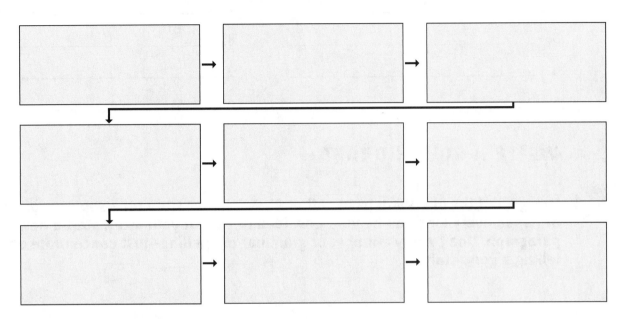

E **What are some specific details you'd like to include in your story?**

1. _____
2. _____
3. _____
4. _____
5. _____

F **What are some thoughts and feelings you'd like to add to make your story more interesting?**

1. _____
2. _____
3. _____
4. _____
5. _____
6. _____

G Look back at the new words you learned in this unit, from the vocabulary pages and from the Academic Word List. What words do you think might fit into your narrative? Make a list of at least ten words below.

1. _____   6. _____

2. _____   7. _____

3. _____   8. _____

4. _____   9. _____

5. _____   10. _____

▶ WRITE A ROUGH DRAFT

H Using all of the ideas you have gathered, write your story on a separate piece of paper. Every time you begin a new idea or part of your story, start a new paragraph. Don't worry about your grammar or spelling—just concentrate on telling a good story.

▶ EDIT THE ROUGH DRAFT: Content

I Look back at your story and answer the following questions.

1. Is my story interesting? _____

   Would someone be interested in reading my story? _____

2. Is my story easy to understand? _____

3. Did I include all the events, details, and thoughts from my brainstorming? _____

4. Did I include some of the new vocabulary words? _____ How many? _____

5. How could I make my story better? _____

   _____

   _____

J Read your story again and make changes based on the questions you answered above.

▶ EDIT THE ROUGH DRAFT: Mechanics

K **Mechanics are the spelling, grammar, and punctuation. Take the following steps to edit the mechanics of your rough draft.**

1. Look at your story and underline any words that you think might be spelled incorrectly. Write them below. Then ask a partner, or look them up in a dictionary, to find the correct spelling.

Unsure of spelling	Correct spelling

2. Make sure every sentence in your story begins with a capital letter and ends with a punctuation mark (., ?, !).

3. Find any phrases or sentences in your story that may have grammar errors. Write them below. Then ask a partner or your teacher for help in correcting them.

Phrase or sentence: _____

Correction: _____

Phrase or sentence: _____

Correction: _____

Phrase or sentence: _____

Correction: _____

Phrase or sentence: _____

Correction: _____

Phrase or sentence: _____

Correction: _____

Phrase or sentence: _____

Correction: _____

Phrase or sentence: _____

Correction: _____

L **Now go back and make the mechanical changes to your story.**

▶ PEER EDITING

Ⓜ Did you give your story a title? If not, write a few ideas.

1. _____   3. _____

2. _____   4. _____

Share your titles with a partner. Which one does your partner like best?

Ⓝ Exchange your story with a partner. Have your partner read your story and answer the following questions. Have your partner underline anything in your story that he or she thinks needs editing.

1. Is the story interesting?
2. Is the story easy to understand?
3. Did the author include some new vocabulary words?
4. Are all the words spelled correctly?
5. Are there any grammar problems?
6. How could this story be better?

Ⓞ Talk to your partner about your story. Go back and make any changes that you think will improve your story.

▶ WRITE THE FINAL PAPER

Ⓟ Write your final paper. Remember the following formatting tips as you write.

1. Put the title at the top center of your paper.
2. Put a space between the title and the first paragraph.
3. Indent the first word of every paragraph.
4. Make sure there are left and right margins on your paper.
5. Write neatly.

Ⓠ Proof your final paper.

▶ Community Challenge

Share your story with at least 5 classmates, family, and friends. If you wrote about your impossible dream, ask them for ideas on how you can make your dream come true.

UNIT 2

Personal Finance

▶ GETTING READY

 A **Discuss the following questions.**

1. At what age do you think you'll retire?
2. Do you currently save money for retirement? If so, how much per year?
3. Where do you/would you keep the money you are saving for retirement?
4. How much money would you like to have when you retire?

B **Look at the chart and answer the questions.**

Contributing $2,000 per year (assuming retirement at age 65)					
	Years of Saving	**Rates of Return**			
Age		**4%**	**6%**	**8%**	**10%**
55 years old	10 years	24,010	26,360	28,970	31,870
45 years old	20 years	59,560	73,570	91,520	114,550
40 years old	25 years	83,290	109,720	146,210	195,690
35 years old	30 years	112,170	158,110	226,560	328,980
30 years old	35 years	147,300	222,860	344,630	542,040
25 years old	40 years	190,050	309,520	518,100	885,160

1. If Marie is 55 years old, how many years of saving does she have left? _____

2. Kendra is 35 years old. If she earns 10% on her money, how much will she have saved when she retires? _____

3. Jackson is a 40-year-old man who plans to retire at age 65 and hopes to earn 10% on his investments. How much will he have saved? _____

4. Find yourself on this chart. Imagine you contribute $2,000 per year to your retirement and hope to earn a 10% return. How much will you have at age 65? _____

A Look at the words. Check (✔) the words that you know.

☐ accumulation ☐ alterations ☐ avoid ☐ coincidence ☐ devoted

☐ essence ☐ forecast ☐ formulate ☐ retire ☐ potential

☐ precisely ☐ rewarding ☐ risk ☐ significantly ☐ speculate

B Replace the underlined word with a word from above.

1. You may have to make <u>changes</u> to your retirement goals as you get older.

   _____

2. Investing when you are young can contribute <u>greatly</u> to what you will have

   for retirement. _____

3. It's no <u>accident</u> that many people who save their money are putting it away

   for retirement. _____

4. That is <u>exactly</u> why some people have no money for retirement. They start saving

   too late. _____

5. I like to get my retirement account statement and see the <u>growth</u>.

   _____

C Read the sentences. Then, write the underlined word next to the correct definition.

1. Young people should <u>avoid</u> putting all of their money into savings accounts.
2. We need to sit down and <u>formulate</u> how much money we'd like to have saved
   for retirement.
3. You should never <u>speculate</u> with something as important as your retirement plan.
4. Based on past financial cycles, financial advisors can <u>forecast</u> the rate of return you
   might get from your investments.
5. I can see myself working at my job for a very long time, so I don't think I will <u>retire</u> early.

   a. _____ say what you think might happen in the future

   b. _____ choose not to do something

   c. _____ buy investments, hoping to sell them later for a
   higher profit

   d. _____ invent a plan, thinking carefully about the details

   e. _____ to leave one's job and stop working completely

D **Read the paragraphs and answer the questions.**

1. Putting all your money in a savings account involves very little risk. You will not lose any money, but you won't make very much money either. In order to take some risks with your retirement funds, you should invest in some stocks or other investments that can make you more money. How do you feel about taking some risks with your retirement money?

_____

_____

2. Investing in the stock market could give you the potential to make a lot of money. You also have the potential to lose a lot of money if the market goes down. What do you do with your money that could give you the potential to make money?

_____

_____

3. Watching your retirement account grow is very rewarding. In other words, it makes you feel good to know that you are saving and making money. Jenna saves $100 from each paycheck. Watching her savings grow is very rewarding to her. What do you do with your money that is rewarding to you?

_____

_____

4. "Retirement planning captures the very essence of financial planning." Therefore, one of the most important reasons to plan financially is to save money so that you can retire comfortably. The _essence_ of something is its basic and most important characteristic that gives it its individual identity. If you have a job, what is the essence of you working . . . to save money for retirement, to pay your bills, to save money for your family, or something else?

_____

_____

► ACADEMIC WORD LIST

E **Which words do you know?**

☐ achieve ☐ affects ☐ aspects ☐ contribute ☐ define

☐ dramatically ☐ economy ☐ enables ☐ enormous ☐ establish

☐ fund ☐ identifying ☐ income ☐ invest ☐ maximize

☐ ongoing ☐ phase ☐ revise ☐ series ☐ strategy

Look at the chart of expressions.

Expression	Definition	Example Sentence
standard of living	the level of comfort and wealth that you have	We are very happy with our standard of living.
nest egg	a sum of money that you are saving for a particular purpose	They have built up a good nest egg to pay for their children's college education.
net worth	the sum of everything you own, minus everything that you owe	Her net worth is so low because even though she owns a house and has a lot of money saved, she owes a lot of money.
get carried away with	to be so exited about something that you do something foolish	He got carried away with investing in stocks and doesn't have any money to put into his retirement account.
put off	to delay doing something	They put off saving for their vacation until it was too late. They had to cancel the trip because they didn't have enough money.
get away with	do something without any negative consequences	I can get away with investing in risky stocks because I have a lot of money invested in low risk investments.

G **Below are things a financial planner might say to you or ask you. Complete each statement or question with a phrase from above.**

1. It is important to build up a good-sized _____ so you can retire comfortably.

2. Saving money for retirement is good but you don't want to _____ saving so much money that you don't have enough to live on.

3. Before we begin, it is important to write down everything you own, every bank account you have, every investment you have, and everything you owe so we can figure out your _____.

4. We enjoy our _____ and would like to keep it when we retire.

5. Can you _____ saving $500 a month? Or is that too much money?

6. Don't _____ saving for retirement or one day you wake up at age 65 and have no money saved.

► DICTIONARY WORK

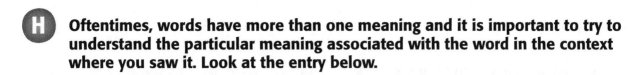

H **Oftentimes, words have more than one meaning and it is important to try to understand the particular meaning associated with the word in the context where you saw it. Look at the entry below.**

> **speculate** /spɛkyəlɪt/ (speculates, speculating, speculated) 1 v If you speculate about something, you make guesses about its nature or identity, or about what might happen. *There's no reason to speculate about why he didn't show up.* 2 v If someone speculates financially, they buy property, stocks, or shares, in the hope of being able to sell them again at a higher price and make a profit. *Ben speculated when he bought that house, but he wasn't able to sell it for a higher price.*

Now look at the sentence from the reading.

You should never speculate with something as important as your retirement plan, but you don't have to totally avoid risk.

Which definition of *speculate* do you think is more appropriate in this context? Why? Do you think it is possible that both definitions could work?

I **Read each sentence below and use your dictionary to find the correct definition of the underlined word. Write the definition.**

1. Once you know what you want out of retirement, the next step is to <u>establish</u> the size of the nest egg you're going to need to achieve your retirement goals.

   Definition: _____

   _____

2. The final step is to <u>formulate</u> an investment program that enables you to build up your required nest egg.

   Definition: _____

   _____

3. Retirement planning would be much simpler if we lived in a static <u>economy</u>.

   Definition: _____

   _____

4. One <u>strategy</u> is to plan for retirement over a series of short-run time frames.

   Definition: _____

   _____

▶ READING CHALLENGE

▶ PRE-READING

A **Work with a small group and brainstorm a list of ways to plan for your retirement.**

Ways to Plan for Retirement

Save $50 every month from my paycheck.

_____

_____

_____

_____

_____

_____

_____

B **Which of the above are you already doing? Put a check (✔) next to each one.**

C **Choose two things from the list above that you would like to start doing to plan for retirement. Write them below.**

EXAMPLE: I would like to start saving money to buy a retirement house.

1. _____

_____

2. _____

_____

D **Complete the statements.**

1. I would like to retire at age _____.

2. When I retire, I would like to live in _____ (city, state, country).

3. When I retire, I would like to have $_____ per month to live on.

4. I could save that much money by doing the following things now:

   a. _____

   b. _____

   c. _____

► **READING**

E **Read the excerpt about retirement planning from *Personal Financial Planning*, a college textbook.**

Role of Retirement Planning in Personal Financial Planning

1. The financial planning process would be incomplete without retirement planning. Certainly no financial goal is more important than achieving a comfortable standard of living in retirement. In many aspects, retirement planning captures the very essence of financial planning. It is forward looking (perhaps more so than any other aspect of financial planning), affects both your current and future standard of living, and, if successful, can be highly rewarding and contribute significantly to your net worth.

2. Okay, so it's important; so where do you start? Well, as with most aspects of financial planning, you need a goal or an objective—that is, the first step in retirement planning is to set goals for yourself. Take some time to define the things you want to do in retirement, the standard of living you hope to maintain, the level of income you'd like to receive, and any special retirement goals you may have (like buying a retirement home in Arizona, or taking an around-the-world cruise). Such goals are important because they give direction to your retirement planning. Of course, like all goals, they're subject to change[1] over time as the situations and conditions in your life change.

3. Once you know what you want out of retirement, the next step is to establish the size of the nest egg you're going to need to achieve your retirement goals. How much money will you need to retire the way you'd like? The final step is to formulate an investment program that enables you to build up your required nest egg. This usually involves creating some type of systematic savings plan (putting away a certain amount of money each year) and identifying the types of investment vehicles[2] that will best meet your retirement needs. This phase of your retirement program is closely related to other aspects of financial planning—investment and tax planning.

4. Investments and investment planning are the vehicles for building up your retirement funds. They're the active, ongoing part of retirement planning in which you manage and invest the funds you've set aside for retirement. It's no coincidence that a major portion of most individual investor portfolios is devoted to building up a pool of funds[3] for retirement. Taxes and tax planning are also important because a major objective of sound retirement planning is to legitimately[4] shield[5] as much income as possible from taxes and, in so doing, maximize the accumulation of retirement funds.

The Three Biggest Pitfalls to Sound Retirement Planning

5. Human nature being what it is, people often get a little carried away with the amount of money they want to build for retirement. Face it, having a nest egg of $4 million or $5 million would be great, but it's beyond the reach of most people. Besides, you don't need that much to live comfortably in retirement. So set a more realistic goal. But when you set that goal, remember: It's not going to happen by itself; you have to do something to bring it about. And this is precisely where things start to fall apart. Why? Because when it comes to retirement planning, people tend to make three big mistakes:
- They start too late.
- They put away too little.
- They invest too conservatively.

[1] **subject to change** – something that is not permanent and most likely will become different
[2] **investment vehicles** – places to invest your money
[3] **pool of funds** – an amount of money
[4] **legitimate** – acceptable according to the law
[5] **shield** – protect

6. Many people in their twenties, or even thirties, find it hard to put money away for retirement. Most often, that's because they have other, more pressing financial concerns—such as buying a house, retiring a student loan, or paying for child care. The net result is that they often put off retirement planning until later in life—in many cases, until they're in their late thirties or forties. Unfortunately, the longer people put it off, the less they're going to have in retirement. Or, they're not going to be able to retire as early as they'd hoped. Even worse, once people start a retirement program, they tend to be too skimpy[6] and put away too little. Although this, too, may be due to pressing[7] family needs, all too often it boils down to[8] lifestyle choices. They'd rather spend for today than save for tomorrow. So, they end up putting maybe $1000 a year into a retirement plan when, with a little more effective financial planning and family budgeting, they could easily afford to save two or three times that amount.

7. On top of all this, many people tend to be far too conservative in the way they invest their retirement money. Too often, people fail to achieve the full potential of their retirement programs because they treat them more like savings accounts than investment vehicles! The fact is, they place way too much of their money into low-yielding,[9] fixed income securities,[10] such as CDs and treasury notes. You should never speculate with something as important as your retirement plan, but you don't have to totally avoid risk. There's nothing wrong with following an investment program that involves a reasonable amount of risk, so long as it results in a correspondingly higher level of return. Caution is fine, but being overly cautious can be very costly in the long run. Indeed, a low rate of return can have an enormous impact on the long-term accumulation of capital[11] and, in many cases, may mean the difference between just getting by or enjoying a comfortable retirement.

Estimating Income Needs

8. Retirement planning would be much simpler if we lived in a static[12] economy. Unfortunately (or perhaps fortunately), we don't, so, both your personal budget and the general state of the economy will change considerably over time. All of which makes accurate forecasting of retirement needs difficult at best. Even so, it's a necessary task and you can handle it in one of two ways. One strategy is to plan for retirement over a series of short-run time frames. A good way to do this is to state your retirement income objectives as a percentage of your present earnings. For example, if you desire a retirement income equal to 80 percent of your final take-home pay, you can determine the amount necessary to fund this need. Then, every 3 to 5 years, you can revise and update your plan.

9. Alternately, you can follow a long-term approach in which you actually formulate the level of income you'd like to receive in retirement, along with the amount of funds you must amass to achieve that desired standard of living. Rather than addressing the problem in a series of short-run plans, this approach goes 20 or 30 years in to the future—to the time when you'll retire—to determine how much saving and investing you must do today to achieve your long-run retirement goals. Of course, if conditions or expectations should happen to change dramatically in the future (as they very likely could), it may be necessary to make corresponding alterations to your long-run retirement goals and strategies.

Personal Financial Planning by Lawrence J. Gitman, CFP and Michael D. Joenk, CFA © 2008

---

[6] **skimpy** – too small in quantity

[7] **pressing** – something that needs immediate attention

[8] **boils down to** – to come to the main point

[9] **low-yielding** – making little interest, as in a savings account that makes 2% interest

[10] **securities** – stocks, shares, bonds, or other certificates that you buy in order to earn regular interest from them or to sell later for a profit

[11] **capital** – a sum of money invested to make more money

[12] **static** – something that does not change

► MAIN IDEAS

F **A paragraph always has a *topic* sentence, a sentence which gives the reader the main idea of the paragraph. Circle the topic sentence for the paragraphs from the reading.**

1. Paragraph 1
   a. Certainly no financial goal is more important than achieving a comfortable standard of living in retirement.
   b. The financial planning process would be incomplete without retirement planning.
   c. In many aspects, retirement planning captures the very essence of financial planning.

2. Paragraph 2
   a. Well, as with most aspects of financial planning, you need a goal or an objective—that is, the first step in retirement planning is to set goals for yourself.
   b. Take some time to define the things you want to do in retirement, the standard of living you hope to maintain, the level of income you'd like to receive, and any special retirement goals you may have.
   c. Such goals are important because they give direction to your retirement planning.

3. Paragraph 3
   a. This phase of your retirement program is closely related to other aspects of financial planning—investment and tax planning.
   b. Once you know what you want out of retirement, the next step is to establish the size of the nest egg you're going to need to achieve your retirement goals.
   c. The final step is to formulate an investment program that enables you to build up your required nest egg.

4. Paragraph 4
   a. It's no coincidence that a major portion of most individual investor portfolios is devoted to building up a pool of funds for retirement.
   b. They're the active, ongoing part of retirement planning in which you manage and invest the funds you've set aside for retirement.
   c. Investments and investment planning are the vehicles for building up your retirement funds.

G **Identify the topic sentences for the following paragraphs and write them below.**

1. Paragraph 5

   _____

   _____

2. Paragraph 6

   _____

   _____

H **Circle the best answer.**

1. According to the reading, what is the most important financial goal?
   a. retirement planning
   b. achieving a comfortable standard of living in retirement
   c. retiring
   d. finding a good financial planner

2. What is the first step in retirement planning?
   a. finding a financial planner
   b. establishing the size of the nest egg you'd like
   c. setting a goal
   d. formulating an investment plan

3. What are the three biggest mistakes people make when planning for retirement?
   a. consulting friends, investing in bonds, and putting away too little
   b. investing in real estate, not using a financial planner, and saving for a retirement house
   c. starting at an early age, paying for child care, and putting money into savings accounts
   d. starting too late, investing too conservatively, and putting away too little

4. Why do many people not achieve the full potential of their retirement savings?
   a. They put all their money into low-yielding, fixed income securities.
   b. They invest in risky stocks.
   c. They have a variety of investments in their portfolio.
   d. They don't save any money.

5. Why will your personal budget change over time?
   a. The interest on your investments may change.
   b. You might get a new job.
   c. We live in an economy that is constantly changing.
   d. Your standard of living will change.

6. What is one way to forecast your retirement needs?
   a. Save every bit you can from your monthly income.
   b. Plan for a certain percentage of your current income and revise as necessary.
   c. Ask your friends how much they plan to retire on.
   d. Change your retirement goals and strategies every year.

► OUTLINE

 An outline contains main points (A, B, C, etc.) and supporting details (1, 2, 3, etc.). Using information from the reading, complete the outline below. (Choose the two most important details.)

I. Three Steps to Retirement Planning
    A. Set goals for yourself.
        1. Take some time to define the things you want to do in retirement, the standard of living you hope to maintain, the level of income you'd like to receive, and any special retirement goals you may have.
        2. These goals may change over time as the situations and conditions in your life change.
    B. Establish the size of the nest egg you're going to need to achieve your retirement goals.
    C. Formulate an investment program that enables you to build up your required nest egg.
        1. _____
        2. _____

II. The Three Biggest Pitfalls to Sound Retirement Planning
    A. They start too late.
        1. _____
        2. _____
    B. _____
        1. _____
        2. _____
    C. _____
        1. People treat their retirement accounts like savings accounts.
        2. _____

III. Two Approaches to Estimating Income Needs
    A. Plan for retirement over a series of short-run time frames
        1. _____
        2. Every 3 to 5 years, you can revise and update your plan.
    B. _____
        1. _____
        2. _____

▶ WRITING CHALLENGE: Process

A A process paragraph is a piece of writing that explains a process, how something is done or how something works. What process was explained in the reading on retirement planning?

B Read the process paragraph that Andres wrote. Then, do the following exercises on a separate piece of paper.

	Our Retirement Plan
	Last year, my wife and I set up our retirement plan. She has been
	asking me ever since we got married to formulate a plan, so we finally did
	it. First, we had to decide how much we wanted for a nest egg. We both
	decided that we'd like to have the same amount of money per month that
	we have now. I really enjoy our current standard of living, and we agreed
	that we'd like that same lifestyle in retirement. Next, we had to decide
	at what age we wanted to retire. We both really enjoy our jobs and are
	in good health so we chose age 65 as our retirement age. That gives us
	about 25 years to build up our retirement accounts. My wife's company
	offers its employees a 401(k), so she has been contributing for the past
	15 years. I own my own business so it's up to me to put money away for
	retirement. After we decided upon our retirement age, we decided to
	contact a financial advisor to help guide us on which investments would
	be best for us. She was very helpful in helping my wife reallocate her
	current 401(k) plan, as well as helping us set some personal investment
	accounts. We couldn't have done it without her guidance. Finally, we
	set up automatic contribution amounts so that we put money into
	each account every month. This way, we know the money is going to
	retirement. Furthermore, we know that if we keep contributing the same
	amounts, we will reach our nest egg goal by the time we retire. Setting
	up our retirement plan was hard work, but it will be worth it in the end!

1. Write Andres's topic sentence.
2. Write an outline for Andres's paragraph. (*Hint:* It has 4 main points (A, B, C, D) and two supporting details (1, 2) for each point.
3. Write Andres's conclusion sentence. (A conclusion sentence is usually the last sentence of a paragraph. It summarizes the paragraph.)

C Transitions are words used to connect ideas. What transitions does Andres use? (*Hint:* First, . . .)

► CHOOSE A TOPIC

D **You will be explaining a process. Choose one of the following topics for your process paragraph. Circle the topic you choose.**

1. Explain what you have done to plan for your retirement.

2. Explain what you would like to do to plan for your retirement.

3. Explain what a friend or family member has done to plan for his or her retirement.

► BRAINSTORM: Ideas for Your Story

E **Come up with ideas for your paragraph and complete the outline below. Come up with at least three main points and two supporting details for each point.**

I. (topic sentence) _____

    A. _____

    _____

       1. _____

       2. _____

    B. _____

    _____

       1. _____

       2. _____

    C. _____

    _____

       1. _____

       2. _____

    D. _____

    _____

       1. _____

       2. _____

F   Now write a conclusion sentence for your paragraph.

_____

_____

G   Look at the list of transition words/phrases below. Circle the ones that you would like to use in your process paragraph.

First	Next	Finally
Second	After	In the end
Third	After that	Ultimately
	Later	

H   Look back at the new words and expressions you learned in this unit, from the vocabulary pages and from the Academic Word List. What words do you think might fit into your process paragraph? Make a list of at least six words/expressions.

1. _____   4. _____

2. _____   5. _____

3. _____   6. _____

▶ WRITE A ROUGH DRAFT

I   Using your outline, transition words, and new vocabulary words/expressions, write your process paragraph on a separate piece of paper. Don't worry about your grammar or spelling. Just concentrate on clearly explaining a process.

▶ EDIT THE ROUGH DRAFT: Content

J   Look back at your paragraph and answer the following questions.

1. Did I explain the process clearly?_____
   Would someone else understand the process? _____
2. Did I include all my main points and details? _____
3. Did I connect my ideas with transitions? _____
4. Did I include some of the new vocabulary words/expressions? _____
   How many? _____
5. How could I make my process paragraph better?

   _____

   _____

K   Read your paragraph again and make any changes based on the questions you answered above.

Now that you have edited the content of your story, it is time to edit the mechanics.

1. Look at your paragraph and underline any words that you think might be spelled incorrectly. Write them below. Then ask a partner or look them up in a dictionary to find the correct spelling.

Unsure of spelling	Correct spelling

2. Make sure every sentence in your story begins with a capital letter and ends with a punctuation mark (., ?, !).

3. Find any phrases or sentences in your story that may have grammar errors. Write them below. Then ask a partner or your teacher for help in correcting them.

Phrase or sentence: _____

Correction: _____

Phrase or sentence: _____

Correction: _____

Phrase or sentence: _____

Correction: _____

Phrase or sentence: _____

Correction: _____

Phrase or sentence: _____

Correction: _____

Phrase or sentence: _____

Correction: _____

Phrase or sentence: _____

Correction: _____

 Now go back and make the mechanical changes to your story.

► PEER EDITING

N   **Did you give your paragraph a title? If not, write down a few ideas.**

1. _____
2. _____

3. _____
4. _____

Share your titles with a partner. Which one does your partner like best?

O   **Now, exchange your paragraph with a partner. Have your partner read your paragraph and answer the following questions. Have your partner underline anything in your paragraph that he or she thinks needs editing.**

1. Did the author include a title?
2. Did the author include a topic sentence?
3. Is the process easy to understand?
4. Did the author use some new vocabulary words?
5. Are all the words spelled correctly?
6. Are there any grammar problems?
7. Did the author use transitions to connect ideas?
8. Did the author end with a conclusion sentence?
9. How could the paragraph be better?

P   **Talk to your partner about your paragraph. Go back and make any changes that you think will improve it.**

► WRITE THE FINAL PAPER

Q   **Write your final paper. Remember the following formatting tips as you write:**

1. Put the title at the top center of your paper.
2. Put a space between the title and the first paragraph.
3. Indent the first word of every paragraph.
4. Make sure there are left and right margins on your paper.
5. Write neatly.

R   **Proof your final paper.**

►Community Challenge

Find more information on retirement planning from a magazine, a newspaper, the television, or a financial advisor. Share what you learn with your classmates.

Automotive Know-How

▶ GETTING READY

A Read the checklist.

> ### How to maintain your automobile
> ✔ Change your air filter
> ✔ Check your oil levels
> ✔ Perform an oil change
> ✔ Perform a timing belt inspection
> ✔ Replace your wipers
> ✔ Perform a radiator flush
> ✔ Check your power steering fluid
> ✔ Inspect your brakes
> ✔ Check and fill your coolant
> ✔ Check and replace your spark plugs
> ✔ Top off your washer fluid
> ✔ Check your wheel bolts

B Each item on the checklist above affects your safety while driving a vehicle. Talk with your classmates and discuss why each of the above maintenance items is important for your safety. Write down some of your ideas.

1. It is important to top off your washer fluids so you can keep your windshield clean. If you can't see well out your windshield you may not see hazards in the road that could cause an accident.

2. _____

   _____

   _____

3. _____

   _____

   _____

▶ VOCABULARY CHALLENGE

A Look at the words. Check (✔) the words that you know.

☐ abrupt   ☐ advance   ☐ strides   ☐ trend   ☐ maximize

☐ eliminating   ☐ detects   ☐ dictate   ☐ distraction   ☐ proximity

☐ innovative   ☐ enable   ☐ selective   ☐ industry   ☐ panic

B Read the sentences. Then, write the underlined word next to the correct definition.

1. Electronic stability control is the most important safety <u>advance</u> to the automobile since the invention of the safety belt.
2. A feeling of <u>panic</u> can be caused by an accident happening right in front of you.
3. The automobile <u>industry</u> has gone a long way to make cars that can protect passengers in a crash.
4. It is not safe to drive in close <u>proximity</u> to another vehicle.
5. Great <u>strides</u>, much faster than expected, have been made in automobile safety in the past five years.
6. The current <u>trend</u> is toward creating technologies for crash prevention.
7. Other passengers talking while you are driving can be a <u>distraction</u>.

   a. _____ rapid progress

   b. _____ development toward something different

   c. _____ progress in understanding something or doing it well

   d. _____ something that takes your attention away from something you are concentrating on

   e. _____ the people and activities involved in making a particular product

   f. _____ strong feelings of anxiety or fear that makes you react without thinking

   g. _____ nearness to a place or person

C Write sentences using each of the nouns above.

1. _____
2. _____
3. _____
4. _____
5. _____
6. _____
7. _____

D **Read the definitions and examples below.**

Verb	Definition	Example sentence
detect	to find or notice something	If the system detects the car beginning to roll-over, it will automatically deploy the air bags.
dictate	for one thing to affect or influence another	The trend toward creating technologies for crash prevention will dictate the new types of safety systems we see in cars.
eliminate	to remove completely	This new tire could eliminate the need to change a tire in bad weather.
enable	to make something possible	A built-in microphone enables the driver to speak with an operator.
maximize	to make something as great in amount or importance as you can	New technology can sense a collision before it is about to happen and maximize the safety of the driver.

E **Read each sentence below and circle the correct word.**

1. New safety systems *detect / eliminate* the need for you to worry while on the road.

2. Computer technology in cars will *detect / enable* when you need to get your oil changed.

3. The backup camera in some cars *eliminates / enables* drivers to see what is behind them when the car is in reverse.

4. Research on how accidents are caused *maximizes / dictates* what safety features the automobile industry tries to implement in new vehicles.

5. Driving without distractions can help *eliminate / maximize* your safety.

F **Match each underlined adjective below to its correct definition.**

1. _____ <u>abrupt</u> stop   a. only applies to certain situations

2. _____ <u>innovative</u> idea   b. new and original

3. _____ <u>selective</u> braking   c. sudden, quick

► **ACADEMIC WORD LIST**

G **Which words do you know?**

☐ adaptive   ☐ adjusting   ☐ approaching   ☐ capability   ☐ potential

☐ constantly   ☐ maintain   ☐ creating   ☐ demonstration   ☐ stability

☐ designed   ☐ ultimately   ☐ display   ☐ minor   ☐ require

☐ image   ☐ impact   ☐ initial   ☐ input   ☐ restraints

H Look at the following expressions. Complete the sentences below.

Expression	Definition
turned up	when someone or something arrives unexpectedly or after you have been waiting a long time
wander off	move away from
just over the horizon	available soon
out of control	having no control
on a smaller scale	not as large or grand as something else
bundled with	comes with

1. A sleepy driver might let his car _____ the road.

2. Once the car hit the guardrail, it spun _____.

3. Many new safety features haven't shown up on cars yet, but they are

   _____.

4. Many new cars are coming _____ a DVD player and a

   navigation system.

5. Advanced safety features can add expense to a car. _____,

   standard features like seat belts and daytime running lights are included.

6. DVDs player have _____ in many "mom cars" as a means

   to keep children occupied.

 Discuss the following questions with a small group.

1. What would you like a car you are buying to come bundled with?
2. What could make your car wander off the road?
3. Have you ever been driving a car when it spun out of control?
4. What new features in cars do you think might be just over the horizon?

► DICTIONARY WORK

J If you know the meaning of one word, you probably know the meaning of all of the other words in its word family. Look at the example below.

Noun	Verb	Adjective	Adverb
selection	select	selective	selectively

K Match each word to its meaning.

1. _____ selection   a. chosen carefully

2. _____ select   b. a choice

3. _____ selective   c. only applying to certain group

4. _____ selectively   d. to choose

L Using your dictionary, complete the chart below with all the words in the word families. (*Note:* Not all words will have all parts of speech.)

Noun	Verb	Adjective	Adverb
distraction			
		innovative	
	detect		
collision			
	adapt		
elimination			
			automatically

M Choose three of the new vocabulary words you have learned in this unit. Look each one up in your dictionary. Write their complete dictionary entries on a separate piece of paper. Then, write an example sentence for each word below.

1. _____

_____

2. _____

_____

3. _____

_____

► **PRE-READING**

A Check (✔) each automobile safety feature that you have heard of.

☐ stability control   ☐ adaptive cruise control
☐ pre-collision systems   ☐ rollover mitigation
☐ lane-departure warning   ☐ active head restraints
☐ brake assist   ☐ voice-recognition technology
☐ blind-spot detection   ☐ intelligent networks
☐ night vision   ☐ backup camera

B What do you think each of the features above are? Discuss with a small group.

C Now, label each picture with the name of the correct safety feature.

1.
_____

5.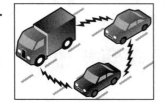
_____

9.
_____

2.
_____

6.
_____

10.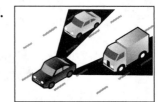
_____

3.
_____

7.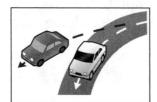
_____

11.
_____

4.
_____

8.
_____

12.
_____

Read the article on Automobile Safety from the April 2007 issue of *Consumer Reports*®.

What's Next in Auto Safety

Innovative advances will soon make driving safer than ever

Electronic stability control (ESC), which selectively applies brakes to one or more wheels when a vehicle is about to slide out of control, is the most important safety advance since the safety belt. Recent studies have found that ESC could save as many as 10,000 lives a year if all cars had the system. Beginning in 2012, the federal government will require that all new cars come equipped[1] with ESC.

On a smaller scale, backup cameras, another safety system that is becoming more common, can now help prevent accidents with children or objects hidden in a vehicle's rear blind zone.[2]

The industry has gone a long way to make cars that can protect passengers in a crash, so now the trend is toward creating technologies for crash prevention. This will dictate the types of new safety systems we will see in mainstream cars. Most of the following have already turned up in limited use and the others appear to be just over the horizon.

Next-generation stability control. New ESC systems will go further in managing vehicle dynamics.[3] One system, ESC II, is designed to provide slight steering input, together with selective braking and throttle reduction,[4] to maintain control. Rear-wheel steering control through an active multilink suspension[5] is also being looked at to work with next-generation ESC, providing optimum stability.

Curtain air bags. Usually mounted[6] in a vehicle's headliner above the windows, curtain air bags deploy[7] across the windows in a crash to protect passengers' heads in both front and rear seats. They also help shield[8] occupants from flying debris,[9] and can keep people from being ejected[10] during a rollover. The better head-protection systems offer a safety-canopy system, which automatically deploys the side-curtain air bags if the system detects the vehicle beginning to roll over.

Pre-collision systems. Currently found on a few vehicles from Mercedes-Benz and Lexus, these sense a collision before it happens and take action to warn the driver and maximize the safety of all the car's occupants. It detects vehicles in front and can sound an alarm and display warning lights. The system then takes preventive steps such as fully charging the brakes and air bags, closing windows, adjusting seat positions for optimal[11] air-bag effectiveness, and activating safety-belt pretensioners.[12] An advanced pre-collision system in the Lexus LS600h L will detect pedestrians and animals on the road as well as other vehicles. And a camera will watch if the driver is not looking ahead at potential road hazards[13] and sound an alert to get his attention if it senses an impending[14] collision.[15]

[1] **equipped** – having the necessary tools/equipment
[2] **blind spot/zone** – an area where you can't see
[3] **dynamics** – opposing forces that cause change
[4] **throttle reduction** – reduce the vehicle speed
[5] **suspension** – springs and devices attached to wheels which give the car a smoother ride
[6] **mounted** – fixed firmly
[7] **deploy** – to spread out, utilize or arrange for a specific purpose
[8] **shield** – protect
[9] **debris** – pieces of unwanted material
[10] **ejected** – removed or pushed out forcefully
[11] **optimal** – the best possible
[12] **safety-belt pretensioners** – a device that tightens the safety belt
[13] **hazards** – something in your way, which could be dangerous
[14] **impending** – happening soon
[15] **collision** – when a moving object crashes into something

Adaptive cruise control. In addition to maintaining a set speed on the highway, this system can automatically maintain a safe distance from the vehicle ahead. It does this by using radar[16] to monitor vehicles in front, and operates the brakes or throttle to slow or accelerate the car as needed. We tested adaptive cruise control in a few vehicles and some of our drivers found the systems to be annoyingly abrupt in their operation. By 2009, Volvo will have a system that works in stop-and-go traffic and will be able to bring a car to a complete stop if necessary.

Lane-departure warning. Cameras that detect the stripes between lanes can determine if a sleepy or inattentive driver has let the vehicle wander off its intended path. The driver is then alerted with a chime and warning light. We tested a system on the Infiniti M35x and found that the chime went off constantly on minor roads. Many of our drivers found it so annoying they turned it off. It was more useful on the freeway.

Brake assist. This system senses when emergency braking is required by gauging[17] how fast the pedal is depressed.[18] When panic braking is detected, brake assist builds up boost[19] to use the vehicle's maximum braking capability even if the driver doesn't push on the pedal hard enough, which might happen in some crash situations.

Blind-spot detection. Many accidents occur when a driver tries to change lanes without being aware that a vehicle is in a blind spot. Audi and Volvo currently have systems that use warning lights connected to cameras or radar on the outside mirrors to tell a driver when a vehicle is in or approaching a blind zone.

Night vision. These systems use infrared technology[20] to allow a driver to see objects, animals, and people well beyond the reach of a car's headlights. We've found them to be useful in some situations, but not ideal. New systems by BMW, Mercedes-Benz, and Lexus might provide a greater range.[21] In the past, we found these systems to be distracting; we hope that the new ones will be less so.

Traction control. Traction control helps keep two-wheel-drive vehicles moving in slippery conditions. If it detects a drive-wheel slipping, it automatically applies a slight amount of brake pressure to that wheel and, if necessary, cuts back on engine power to stop the slipping. Traction control can also send power to whichever drive wheel has the most grip.[22] But if neither drive wheel has grip, traction control won't help. While ultimately not as good as all-wheel drive or four-wheel drive in extreme conditions, traction control may be all you need in light rain or snow. It is especially helpful on rear-wheel-drive vehicles.

Rollover mitigation. Roll sensors augment[23] stability control and determine if the vehicle is tipping up on two wheels. If an impending rollover is detected, stability control applies selective braking to suppress[24] the roll motion. If that fails, curtain air bags are deployed and stay inflated for about six seconds to protect occupants from possible impact[25] and to help keep them from being ejected.

Active head restraints. This technology moves the restraints behind a person's head forward during a collision to help absorb energy and prevent whiplash injuries. Neck injuries are the most common kind reported in auto crashes and tests have shown that good head restraints, especially active ones, are effective in preventing them.

---

[16] **radar** – radio signals which help discover the position or speed of objects
[17] **gauging** – measuring or judging something
[18] **depressed** – pushed down
[19] **boost** – energy
[20] **infrared technology** – special equipment that allows one to see radiation (radiation is similar to light but has a longer wavelength)
[21] **range** – the maximum area in which things can be reached or detected
[22] **grip** – firm hold
[23] **augment** – to make something larger, stronger, or more effective
[24] **suppress** – prevent
[25] **impact** – the action of one object hitting another

Voice recognition. These systems already exist in some higher-end vehicles, where you can use them to control the climate, audio, cell-phone, and navigation systems.[26] Early versions were cumbersome[27] to use and had difficulties recognizing voice commands, but the technology has made great strides. Some voice-recognition systems are now used with Bluetooth technology, which pairs up your cellular phone to the car's audio system. Using voice commands instead of buttons, knobs, and touch screens should reduce driver distraction, which could in turn reduce accidents.

Proximity warning systems. Offered on a few Volvo models, proximity warning systems alert inattentive drivers before they rear-end another car. Proximity warning systems are only available on cars equipped with adaptive[28] cruise control, as they use the same radar. If you come up behind another car too quickly, the system sounds an alert and flashes a red light at the base of the windshield. If you still don't slow down, the Volvo system can apply the car's brakes to avoid or reduce an impact.

Backup cameras. Cameras that send an image to a dashboard-mounted screen when you shift into reverse are becoming increasingly common. Available on many cars, trucks, and SUVs, these cameras add a measure of safety, particularly on larger vehicles with big blind spots. *Consumer Reports* testing has shown that for shorter drivers in some of the worst vehicles, a small child can't be seen when less than 70 feet from the rear bumper. Cameras show what's immediately behind the cars, which also makes them handy for hooking up a trailer. The downside is that cameras often come bundled with navigation systems, and they can add $2,000 or more to the sticker price.[29]

Run-flat tires. Tires that can maintain their shape and can be driven on for 50 miles or more with no air in them are becoming increasingly common on some new vehicles. More than just a convenience item, run-flats can add a degree of security by eliminating the need to change a tire in bad weather or dangerous roadside areas. But their stiff sidewalls[30] can deliver a harsher[31] ride. And some owners have complained of premature wear and high replacement cost.

Vehicle telematics. The combination of telecommunications and computing technology is becoming more common in new cars. The most common system is General Motors' OnStar system, which is now standard on many GM vehicles (it's a subscription service after an initial demonstration period.). Also, marketed by Lexus, OnStar allows drivers to speak with an operator in an emergency by simply pushing a button. If the vehicle sends a signal that it has been in an accident, an operator can call to check on you. A built-in microphone and the car's stereo speakers enable the motorist[32] to speak with an operator. Other manufacturers including Mercedes-Benz and Acura have their own telematics systems.

---

[26] **navigation systems** – computing technology that gives maps and directions
[27] **cumbersome** – complicated and inefficient
[28] **adaptive** – able to change in order to deal with new situations
[29] **sticker price** – price a dealer charges for a car
[30] **stiff sidewalls** – the side of a tire which is hard and sturdy
[31] **harsh** – rough
[32] **motorist** – a person who drives a car

▶ MAIN IDEA

E **Match the safety system with its description.**

1. _____ active head restraints

2. _____ air bags

3. _____ backup cameras

4. _____ blind-spot detection

5. _____ brake assist

6. _____ cruise control

7. _____ lane-departure warning

8. _____ night vision

9. _____ pre-collision systems

10. _____ proximity warning systems

11. _____ rollover mitigation

12. _____ run-flat tires

13. _____ stability control

14. _____ traction control

15. _____ vehicle telematics

16. _____ voice recognition

a. maintains a safe distance from vehicle in front

b. a safety bag that deploys to protect one's head

c. the combination of telecommunication and computing technology which allows the occupants to speak with an operator

d. helps keep the vehicle moving in slippery conditions

e. applies brakes when vehicle is about to slide out of control

f. a warning light that indicates when a vehicle is approaching a blind zone

g. determines if the vehicle is tipping up on two wheels

h. a warning light and a sound go off when the vehicle wanders off its intended path

i. moves the restraints during a collision to help prevent whiplash

j. tires that can maintain their shape with no air in them

k. senses a collision before it happens

l. allows the driver to use voice commands to control things such as the climate, the radio, and cell phone

m. allows a driver to see objects beyond the reach of the car's headlights

n. alerts the driver before he or she rear-ends another car

o. a camera in the rear of the vehicle that sends an image to a screen that the driver can see when he or she is in reverse

p. senses when emergency braking is required

F **Complete the following exercises about the main ideas.**

1. What is the main idea of the reading?

   _____

   _____

2. In your own words, describe to a partner how each safety systems works.

3. Number each safety system in order of importance to you.

_____ active head restraints   _____ pre-collision systems

_____ air bags   _____ proximity warning systems

_____ backup cameras   _____ rollover mitigation

_____ blind-spot detection   _____ run-flat tires

_____ brake assist   _____ stability control

_____ cruise control   _____ traction control

_____ lane-departure warning   _____ vehicle telematics

_____ night vision   _____ voice recognition

4. Now share your list with a partner. Are the same things important to you?

▶ **SUPPORTING DETAILS**

G **Supporting details give more information about the main ideas. Look back at the reading and find the supporting details. Write them in your own words below.**

EXAMPLE: Active head restraints. This technology moves the restraints behind a person's head forward during a collision to help absorb energy and prevent injuries.

a. _Neck injuries are the most common in car accidents._

b. _Tests show that quality active head restraints can help prevent these types of neck injuries._

1. Curtain air bags deploy across the windows in a crash to protect the passengers' heads.

   a. _____

   b. _____

   c. _____

2. Roll sensors augment stability control and determine if the vehicle is tipping up on two wheels.

   a. _____

   b. _____

3. Tires that can maintain their shape and be driven on for 50 miles or more with no air in them are becoming more common.

   a. _____

   b. _____

   c. _____

4. Brake assist senses when emergency braking is required by gauging how fast the pedal is depressed.

   a. _____

5. Voice recognition systems already exist in some higher-end vehicles, where you can use them to control the climate, audio, cell-phone, and navigation systems.

   a. _____

   b. _____

   c. _____

H **A good way to explain an idea is to use a real-life example. In the article, examples of safety systems that can be found on certain vehicles manufactured today are given. For example:** Currently found on a few vehicles from Mercedes-Benz and Lexus, these sense a collision before it happens and take action to warn the driver and maximize the safety of all the car's occupants.

Find other examples from the reading and underline them. List the safety systems and the cars they can be found in below.

Safety System	Automobile
pre-collision systems	Mercedes-Benz, Lexus

▶ **EXTENSION**

I **The *Consumer Reports*® article is missing a conclusion paragraph. Write 1–3 sentences below to conclude the article.**

_____

_____

_____

_____

_____

_____

A A summary is a piece of writing that gives all the main ideas from another piece of writing you've read. When writing a summary, it is important to restate the main ideas in your own words. What do you think the purpose of writing a summary is?

B Read the summary below.

> Electronic Stability Control
>
> According to the *Consumer Reports*® article, "What's Next in Auto Safety" (April 2007), one of the most innovative safety advances in recent years is electronic stability control (ESC). Stability control helps keep the car from sliding out of control. It works in a variety of ways. Current ESC works by applying the brakes to certain wheels in the event that the car starts sliding. Other forms of ESC help the car steer, as well as reducing the gas given to the engine. Another possible innovation is helping the car steer with its rear wheels. All of these features combined would give vehicles much more stability than they have today. ESC is going to become required in 2012. It could save thousands of lives.

C In order to write an effective summary you must clearly understand what you have read and be able to put the main ideas into your own words. Compare the summary above to the paragraphs on Electronic Stability Control from p. 39.

► **CHOOSE A TOPIC**

D Without looking back at the *Consumer Reports*® article, try to remember some of the safety features mentioned. List five below.

_____

_____

_____

_____

_____

E Of the five safety features you wrote on the previous page, which one do you understand the best? Circle the feature.

▶ **BRAINSTORM: Ideas for Your Summary**

F Look at the part of the reading that describes the safety feature you've chosen. Write each main idea from the article below (copy the words from the article). Then rewrite each idea in your own words.

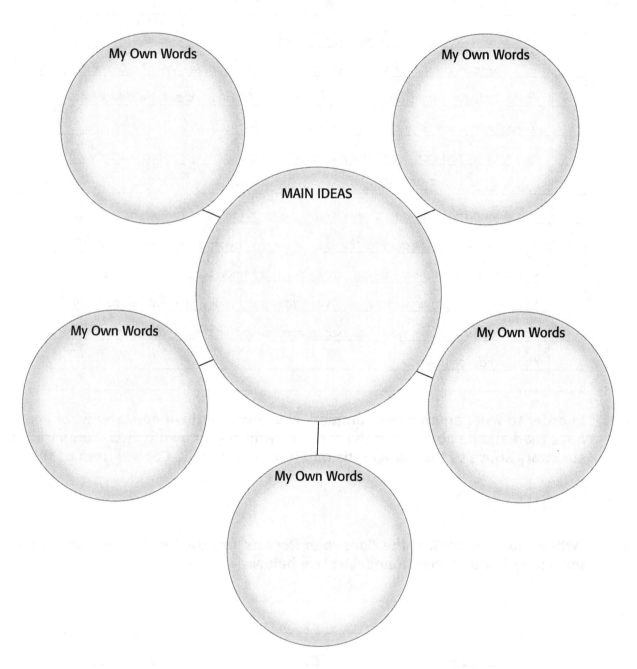

My Own Words

My Own Words

MAIN IDEAS

My Own Words

My Own Words

My Own Words

G **Look at the topic sentence from the example summary.**

According to the Consumer Reports® article, "What's Next in Auto Safety" (April 2007), one of the most innovative safety advances in recent years is electronic stability control (ESC).

It is important to include the source where you got your information from, in this case *Consumer Reports®*. Write your own topic sentence below.

_____

_____

_____

H **Look back at the new words you learned in this unit, from the vocabulary pages and from the Academic Word List. What words do you think might fit into your narrative? Make a list of at least five words below.**

1. _____   4. _____

2. _____   5. _____

3. _____

▶ **WRITE A ROUGH DRAFT**

I **Using all of the ideas you have gathered, write your summary on a separate piece of paper. Start with your topic sentence. Make sure to use transitions to connect your ideas. Do not worry about your grammar or spelling. Just concentrate on writing a good summary.**

▶ **EDIT THE ROUGH DRAFT: Content**

J **Look back at your paragraph and answer the following questions.**

1. Does my summary make sense?_____

   Would someone else understand my summary?_____

2. Did I include all the main ideas from my brainstorming? _____

3. Did I include a topic sentence? _____

4. Did I include some of the new vocabulary words? _____

   How many? _____

5. How could I make my summary better?

   _____

K **Read your summary again and make changes based on the questions you answered above.**

▶ EDIT THE ROUGH DRAFT: Mechanics

 Now that you have edited the content of your story, edit the mechanics. Take the following steps to edit the mechanics of your rough draft.

1. Look at your summary and underline any words that you think may be spelled incorrectly. Write them below. Then ask a partner, or look them up in a dictionary, to find the correct spelling.

Unsure of Spelling	Correct Spelling

2. Make sure every sentence in your story begins with a capital letter and ends with a punctuation mark (., ?, !).

3. Find any phrases or sentences in your story that may have grammar errors. Write them below. Then ask a partner or your teacher for help in correcting them.

Phrase or sentence: _____

Correction: _____

Phrase or sentence: _____

Correction: _____

Phrase or sentence: _____

Correction: _____

Phrase or sentence: _____

Correction: _____

M **Now go back and make the mechanical changes to your story.**

▶ PEER EDITING

Ⓝ Now, exchange your summary with a partner. Have your partner read your summary and answer the following questions. Have your partner underline anything in your summary that he or she thinks needs editing.

1. Is the summary easy to understand?
2. Did the author include a title?
3. Did the author include a topic sentence that mentions the source?
4. Did the author use some new vocabulary words?
5. Are all the words spelled correctly?
6. Are there any grammar problems?
7. Did the author use transitions to connect ideas?
8. Did the author end with a conclusion sentence?
9. How could the summary be better?

Ⓞ Talk to your partner about your story and go back and make any changes that you think will improve your story.

▶ WRITE THE FINAL PAPER

Ⓟ Write your final paper. Remember the following formatting tips as you write.

1. Put the title at the top center of your paper.
2. Put a space between the title and the first paragraph.
3. Indent the first word of every paragraph.
4. Make sure there are left and right margins on your paper.
5. Write neatly.

Ⓠ Proof your final paper.

▶ Community Challenge

Find a newspaper article or a television news story and write a summary.

UNIT 4

Housing

▶ **GETTING READY**

A What are the differences between the two cities above? Which one would you rather live in? Why?

► VOCABULARY CHALLENGE

A **Look at the words. Check (✔) the words that you know.**

☐ amenities   ☐ assimilated   ☐ boasts   ☐ civilization   ☐ commutes

☐ deemed   ☐ entities   ☐ equipped   ☐ innovation   ☐ priorities

☐ reside   ☐ resources   ☐ shack   ☐ supply   ☐ tradeoffs

B **Read the sentences. Determine which part of speech (noun or verb) the underlined word is and write it on the line. Then, write the underlined word next to the correct definition.**

1. Their family of 6 lives in a two-bedroom <u>shack</u>. _____ Noun _____

2. He <u>resides</u> in a city where the crime rate is very high. _____

3. Some people like to live out in the country, away from <u>civilization</u>. _____

4. She <u>commutes</u> 100 miles to work every day. _____

5. We have <u>assimilated</u> into our new community. _____

6. When we moved, our <u>priorities</u> were safety and plenty of parks. _____

    a. _____ the state of having an advanced level of social organization and a comfortable way of life

    b. _____ to travel a long distance to work every day

    c. _____ a simple hut built from tin, wood, or other materials

    d. _____ to become an accepted part of a community

    e. _____ the things that are most important to you

    f. _____ to live or stay somewhere

C **Answer the following questions.**

1. What would be your top priority if you were looking for a new community to move to?

    _____

2. Where do you reside? _____

3. How long do you commute to school every day? _____

4. Do you feel like you've assimilated into this country? Why or why not? _____

    _____

5. Do you know anyone who lives in a shack? _____

D Read the paragraph below. How would you define each of the underlined words? Write your ideas on the lines after each word.

   The Jones family moved into a new house with great <u>amenities</u>: air-conditioning, hardwood floors, vaulted ceilings, and a large backyard with a pool. The house also came <u>equipped</u> with built-in appliances. The city they moved into <u>boasts</u> being the safest in the country with almost no crime. The Jones family has <u>deemed</u> this house to be the one they will live in for the rest of their lives.

1. amenities _____

2. equip _____

3. boast _____

4. deem _____

Check a dictionary to see if you were right.

E Read the definitions and examples below.

Word	Definition	Example sentence
entities	an organization that exists separately from other things and has a clear identity of its own	There are many entities that rate cities throughout the United States.
resources	materials, money, and other things that can be used	Some small towns may seem attractive, but have limited resources.
innovation	a new thing or new method of doing something	A city with a lot of innovation could bring a lot of money into the community.
supply	to give someone something they want or need	Kokomo is a town that supplies many jobs to its residents.
tradeoff	an exchange of one thing in return for another	There are tradeoffs to living in a city with warm weather all year round.

F Circle the correct word in each sentence.

1. They moved into a neighborhood with amazing *amenities / tradeoffs.*

2. That city likes to *deem / boast* about its large parks and recreation facilities.

3. The *tradeoff / innovation* for low crime in our community is a lack of diversity.

4. The lake nearby *equips / supplies* our town with much-needed water.

5. Many *amenities / entities* have rated our city the most polluted in the world.

6. The problem with living in a big city is that we run out of *innovations / resources* quickly.

G Look at the following expressions. Answer the questions that follow.

Expression	Definition
long for	If you long for something, you want it very much.
planned community	Planned communities are planned out before they are built, including housing, parks, golf courses, recreational facilities, lakes, office parks, and commercial centers.
raise eyebrows	If something causes you to raise an eyebrow, it causes you to feel surprised or disapproving.

1. I long for a house out in the country where there are no streetlights and I can wake up to the sounds of nature. What type of house do you long for? _____

   _____

2. If I could design a planned community and put all my favorite things in it, it would include:

   _____

   _____

   _____

3. Since we live in a small, quiet farming community where local businesses are highly supported, it raised eyebrows all over town when that fast-food restaurant was allowed to move in. What would raise eyebrows in your community? _____

   _____

▶ ACADEMIC WORD LIST

H Which words do you know?

☐ apparently   ☐ approximately   ☐ community   ☐ constant   ☐ definitely

☐ diverse   ☐ environment   ☐ facilities   ☐ features   ☐ income

☐ issues   ☐ location   ☐ nevertheless   ☐ obvious   ☐ overall

☐ publication   ☐ range   ☐ requires   ☐ residents   ☐ sufficient

▶ DICTIONARY WORK

I You can use the information you learn from the dictionary to make vocabulary cards. Look at the sample vocabulary card below:

assimilate	**Translation:** asimilar **Definition:** (v) to become accepted into a community **Sample sentence:** It was difficult for the immigrants to assimilate into their new community. **My sentence:** We assimilated into our new school very quickly. **Word family:** assimilated, assimilating, assimilation
(front of card)	(back of card)

J Answer the questions about the card above.

1. How many vocabulary words should you put on a card? _____

2. What word is on this card? _____

3. What is the translation for this word in your language? _____

4. What part of speech is this word? _____

5. What is the definition of this word? _____

_____

K Choose one of the new words you learned in this unit. Make a vocabulary card below.

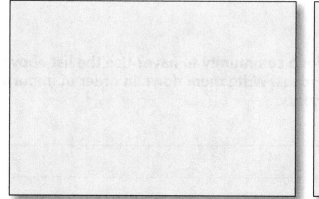

(front of card)	(back of card)

L Choose five of the new vocabulary words you have learned in this unit. Use 4x6 note cards to make vocabulary cards.

> **Suggestion:** Punch a hole in the corner of your card and keep all your cards on a metal ring so you can study them.

► **PRE-READING**

A "Home is where the heart is" is a popular expression. What does this expression mean to you? Discuss with a small group.

B Think about the community you live in. Look at the list below and circle what you think is true about your community.

safe	nightlife	high crime
good weather	good for children	good public transportation
reasonable housing prices	low crime	good schools
employment opportunities		

C Many of the ideas above start with the word *good.* What do the following mean to you?

1. good weather _____

2. good for children _____

3. good public transportation _____

4. good schools _____

D Now share your ideas with a partner. Do they mean the same thing to each of you?

E What do you think is important for a community to have? Use the list above and come up with some of your own ideas. Write them down in order of importance, with number 1 being your top priority.

1. _____

2. _____

3. _____

4. _____

5. _____

READING

F **Read.**

Home Is Where The Heart Is

The Beverly Hillbillies in its nine seasons was deemed as one of the most popular TV sitcoms in the 60s. It centered on Jed Clampett and his family who lived in the backwoods of Tennessee away from civilization. They lived in a small one-bedroom shack with no running water, no heat or air conditioning, no electricity, and dirt floors. Instead of shopping at stores, they hunted small animals to eat and caught fish in a pond close to their home. Jed, while hunting, discovered oil on their property and suddenly was 95 million dollars richer. They loaded up their truck, travelled to Beverly Hills, California, and moved into a spacious mansion equipped with all the amenities. The grandmother, affectionately called "Granny," was able to cook in a large commercial kitchen, the cupboards were always full, and the finely manicured[1] front yard cried of opulence.[2] The family had everything anyone could ever ask for. The only problem—the Clampetts longed for their old home, bugs, wild animals, and all! They even built a small shack out by the cement pond (their swimming pool) to remind them of home.

Where is the best place to live, and how do we choose the best location for us? There are many entities that rate cities throughout the United States. Take for example *CNN Money Magazine.* This publication rates Irvine, California, as the fourth best city in the United States for 2008. Certainly, Irvine boasts of wonderful schools, parks, and recreational facilities.[3] There are 18 large community parks with many features including dog trails, amphitheaters,[4] athletic facilities, handball and tennis courts, and ball diamonds. The community parks range from 10 to 37 acres. The 35 neighborhood parks are smaller and all but one are less than 10 acres. Irvine parks cover an amazing 487 acres. The low crime rate may also be attractive to many. Although Irvine is not one of the top 100 cities in the nation for lowest crime rate, it is nearly 7 times lower than the national average in violent crimes and over 2 times lower than the national average in property crime in 2008.

Irvine is a bit large for those who like small towns, however. The population will climb[5] to over 200,000 in the next few years. It is a planned community that covers approximately 65 square miles. The city webpage speaks of community, but for some, it is hard to have a feeling of community when you don't know most of the people residing in your hometown. Not just anyone can afford to live in such a place. According to *Money Magazine,* the median home price[6] in 2008 was $650,000. The city may be great for those earning $200,000 a year or more, but it is a bit high for the average American. Is Irvine the place for you or are you looking for someplace more affordable with fewer people . . . a small town maybe?

Small is a relative term. There are towns with a few hundred people and others with a few thousand. Kokomo, Indiana might be considered small if compared to Irvine, California. Fewer than 50,000 people live there. The air is clean and residents are reportedly friendly and happy. But the home prices will raise the most eyebrows. An average house costs under $95,000. That's nearly the cheapest in the country and most definitely more affordable than Irvine. But is there employment? Kokomo is known as the "City of Firsts": first in manufacturing, first in innovation, and first in various other things, supplying many jobs to its residents. Although there seems to be work for everyone, if you move there, you will most likely make only $25,000 or $30,000 dollars a year.

[1] **finely manicured** – very short, neatly cut
[2] **opulence** – looking grand or expensive
[3] **recreational facilities** – places to play sports
[4] **amphitheaters** – outdoor theaters
[5] **climb** – increase
[6] **median home price** – average home price

It seems that the safest city is not the cheapest, and the cheapest is not the smallest. The home prices in the cities with good schools might be higher than those with average schools. Big cities tend to have more crime and cities with beautiful landscapes don't always have sufficient employment for the population or the employment requires extended commutes. Apparently there are always tradeoffs. Priorities for one family are often completely different from the priorities for another. Housing, employment, taxes, income, weather, recreation and entertainment, schools, crime (or the lack of it), and various other diverse issues could be considered when choosing a place to live.

Another issue to tackle is how to determine the safest, cheapest, or best city for you. Is the safest the city with the least crime per capita[7] or the least crime overall? Safe might mean the city with the fewest natural disasters like earthquakes or tornadoes. Is the city with the best weather the one with no obvious seasons where the weather is a constant 70 degrees in the middle of the day month in and month out, or where the seasons change from a colorful autumn to a beautiful white winter? Is a city considered large with 50,000, 200,000, or a million people? These questions are personal ones and must be left up to those considering a move. Some cities like Irvine are planned. You can't paint your house any color you want and you must keep your yard pristine.[8] Some small towns may seem attractive, but have limited resources. You might have to travel many miles to find a shopping center or a building contractor. Is there a perfect city for you, or for anyone?

Although the Clampetts never assimilated to their new environment, they found joy because they were with family and they developed friendships in Beverly Hills. "Home is where the heart is" expresses the deep emotion by many who find their heart drawn towards family, friends, or childhood memories. Maybe it doesn't matter where we live as long as we have loved ones close by. The ideal place to live might only exist in our minds; nevertheless, many Americans spend a lifetime looking for such a place when it is probably around them every day.

---

[7] **per capita** – the total amount of something divided by the number of people that live in that area
[8] **pristine** – extremely clean or new

G **Write *True* or *False* on the line. Rewrite the false statements and make them true.**

1. *CNN Money Magazine* rates Irvine, CA as the fifth best city in the U.S. for 2008. _____

   _____

2. Irvine has 35 neighborhood parks. _____

   _____

3. In 2008, the median home price in Irvine was $95,000. _____

   _____

4. Fewer than 40,000 people live in Kokomo, Indiana. _____

   _____

5. Irvine is known as the "City of Firsts." _____

   _____

6. People in Kokomo make over $200,000 a year. _____

   _____

7. The Clampetts never assimilated to their new environment in Beverly Hills. _____

   _____

H **Answer the questions.**

1. Why did the Clampetts move to Beverly Hills? _____

2. How many community parks does Irvine have? _____

3. How many square miles does Irvine cover? _____

4. What does the average house in Kokomo cost? _____

5. How many people live in Kokomo? _____

6. What can't you do to your house in Irvine? _____

7. What two things was Kokomo first in? _____

8. Is Irvine one of the top 100 cities with the lowest crime rate? _____

▶ DESCRIPTION

I **The reading involved descriptions of various homes and cities. Go back and find descriptions of the following places. The first one has been started for you.**

1. Beverly Hillbillies' old home: _____ small, one-bedroom shack _____

_____

_____

_____

2. Beverly Hillbillies' new home: _____

_____

_____

_____

3. Irvine, CA: _____

_____

_____

_____

4. Kokomo, IN: _____

_____

_____

_____

▶ MAIN IDEAS

J **Answer the questions.**

1. Why did the Clampetts long for their old home? _____

_____

2. Why do you think Irvine was rated one of the best cities in the United States?

_____

_____

3. What makes Irvine a planned community? _____

_____

4. Why is Kokomo an attractive place to live? _____

_____

5. Why do you think big cities tend to have more crime? _____

_____

6. Why do you think small towns have limited resources? _____

_____

► OPINION

K **Do you agree or disagree with the following statements? Circle your answer.**

1.	The safest city is not the cheapest city.	agree	disagree
2.	The cheapest city is not the smallest.	agree	disagree
3.	Big cities have more crime.	agree	disagree
4.	Cities with beautiful landscapes don't have sufficient employment.	agree	disagree
5.	Safe means the city with the fewest natural disasters.	agree	disagree
6.	The best weather is 70 degrees all year long.	agree	disagree
7.	A large city has 100,000 people.	agree	disagree
8.	Home is where the heart is.	agree	disagree

L **Share your answers with a partner. Discuss the ones that you disagreed on.**

► SUMMARY

M **Recall what you learned about writing summaries and write a summary of one of the paragraphs from the reading.**

_____

_____

_____

_____

_____

_____

_____

_____

_____

_____

► WRITING CHALLENGE: Description

A A descriptive paragraph is a piece of writing that describes how something or someone looks or feels.

B Read the descriptive paragraph that Janie wrote.

My Ideal Home
If I could live anywhere in the world, I would choose Boulder, Colorado.
I have been there only a handful of times but every time I have gone, I
wished I could stay longer. First of all, the weather is perfect. In the
summer, it is warm and breezy. In the winter, it is cold and snowy.
In my opinion this is the best of both worlds. Second, there are so
many things to do: hiking, biking, skiing, and shopping. Third, it is a
somewhat small city (a little over 100,000 residents), so I always get
a small community feel when I'm there. And finally, the University of
Colorado is located there so there are many employment opportunities.
I have always wanted to work at a big university, and living in Boulder
would give me the perfect chance. Making a move is a big decision, but I
know if I moved to Boulder I would never regret it.

C Answer the questions about Janie's paragraph.

1. What is she describing?

   _____

2. How many main points does she have?

   _____

3. What do you think is most important to Janie in a community?

   _____

► CHOOSE A TOPIC

D Choose one of the topics below and circle it.

1. Describe the community you live in and why you like it.

2. Describe the community you live in and why you don't like it.

3. Describe a community you would like to live in.

► BRAINSTORM: Ideas for Your Description

E Write your topic sentence in the middle circle. Then, write your main points in the outside circles. Try to brainstorm as many main points as you can, but choose only three or four to include in your final paragraph.

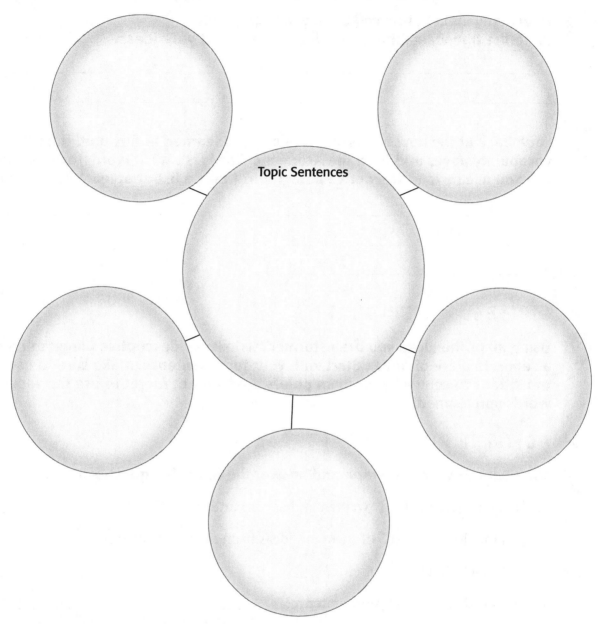

Topic Sentences

F Based on all the information you brainstormed above, write a conclusion sentence for your descriptive paragraph.

_____

_____

_____

_____

G Look back at Janie's paragraph that she wrote on Boulder. What transitions did she use to connect her ideas? Write them below.

_____   _____

_____   _____

H How many main points will be in your paragraph? _____
Write the transitions that you will use to connect your ideas.

_____   _____

_____   _____

I Look back at the new words/expressions you learned in this unit, from the vocabulary pages and from the Academic Word List. What words/expressions can you use in your descriptive paragraph? Make a list of at least five below.

1. _____   4. _____

2. _____   5. _____

3. _____

▶ WRITE A ROUGH DRAFT

J Using all of the ideas you brainstormed, write your descriptive paragraph on a separate piece of paper. Start with your topic sentence. Make sure to use transitions to connect your main points. And, do not forget to use the vocabulary words you learned!

▶ EDIT THE ROUGH DRAFT: Content

K Look back at your paragraph and answer the following questions.

1. Is my paragraph clearly written and easy to understand? _____

2. Did I include at least 3 of the main ideas from my brainstorming? _____

3. Did I include a topic sentence? _____

4. Did I include a conclusion sentence? _____

5. Did I give my paragraph a title? _____

6. Did I include some of the new vocabulary words? _____ How many? _____

7. How could I make my paragraph better? _____

_____

L Read your rough draft again and make changes based on the questions you answered above.

► **EDIT THE ROUGH DRAFT: Mechanics**

M **Now that you have edited the content of your story, edit the mechanics.**

1. Read each statement below.
2. As you read it, check your paragraph.
3. If you answer *no* to any of the statements, try to go back and make the corrections yourself. If you need help, ask a partner or your teacher for help in correcting them.

✔ EDITING CHECKLIST

	Yes	No
The first word of my title is capitalized.	☐	☐
Every word in my title is capitalized (except for small words: a, an, the, in, etc.).	☐	☐
The first letter of every sentence is capitalized.	☐	☐
Every sentence ends with a punctuation mark.	☐	☐
Every sentence has a subject and a verb.	☐	☐
The subject and the verb agree in every sentence.	☐	☐
All of the words are spelled correctly.	☐	☐

► **PEER EDITING**

 N **Now, exchange your paragraph with a partner. Have your partner read your paragraph and use the same checklist above to help you make mechanical changes to your paragraph.**

O Have your partner answer the following questions about your paragraph.

1. Is the paragraph clear and easy to understand?
2. Did the author include a title?
3. Did the author include a topic sentence that explains what the paragraph will be about?
4. Did the author include at least three main points?
5. Did the author add some supporting details to better explain each main point?
6. Did the author use transitions to connect the main points?
7. Did the author use some new vocabulary words?
8. Did the author end with a conclusion sentence?
9. How could the paragraph be better?

P Talk to your partner about your paragraph and go back and make any changes that you think will improve it.

▶ WRITE THE FINAL PAPER

Q Write your final paper. Remember the following formatting tips as you write.

1. Put the title at the top center of your paper.
2. Put a space between the title and the first paragraph.
3. Indent the first word of every paragraph.
4. Make sure there are left and right margins on your paper.
5. Write neatly.

R Proof your final paper.

▶ Community Challenge

Research a place you would like to live. Report what you find out to the class.

UNIT 5 Health

► GETTING READY

A Read the pie chart and information below.

Insurance Coverage in the United States in 2008

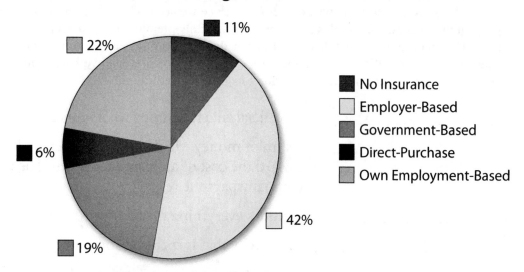

11%

22%

6%

19%

42%

- ■ No Insurance
- □ Employer-Based
- ▨ Government-Based
- ■ Direct-Purchase
- ▨ Own Employment-Based

- Employer-based plans—coverage offered through one's own employment or by a union.
- Government-based health insurance—coverage funded by governments at the federal, state, or local level, such as Medicare, Medicaid, the State Children's Health Insurance Program (SCHIP), military health care, state plans, and the Indian Health Service.
- Direct-purchase plans—coverage through a plan purchased by an individual from a private company.
- Own Employment-based plans—coverage offered through one's own employment and only the policyholder is covered by the plan.

Source: **U.S. Census Bureau, Current Population Survey, 2008 Annual Social and Economic Supplement.**

B Answer the questions with a partner.

1. How are most people in the United States insured?
2. Which type of insurance do the fewest people have?
3. What percentage of people don't have insurance?
4. What percentage of people have their own insurance, either through direct purchase or because they own their own business?
5. Based on the data in the chart, what is the best way for you to get insurance coverage?
6. Where do you fit on the chart?

▶ VOCABULARY CHALLENGE

A **Look at the words. Check (✔) the words that you know.**

☐ compensate ☐ deductible ☐ comprehensive ☐ mandate ☐ expenditures

☐ incentives ☐ obtained ☐ premium ☐ preventative ☐ probability

☐ reductions ☐ referral ☐ reimburse ☐ restriction ☐ surgical

B **Read the paragraph about health insurance. Then write the underlined words next to the correct definition.**

Our family has private health insurance that we pay for on our own. We have a <u>comprehensive</u> policy that covers almost any type of medical service we need. The only <u>restriction</u> is on cosmetic <u>surgical</u> procedures, such as plastic surgery. Our monthly <u>premium</u> is $250. Our annual <u>deductible</u> is $2,000, so once we've met that, all of our medical <u>expenditures</u> are completely covered by the insurance company. We try to make sure we get plenty of <u>preventative</u> care (annual checkups, dental cleaning, eye exams, etc.) so we don't incur huge medical bills.

1. _____ an official rule that limits what you can do

2. _____ a sum of money which an insured person has to pay toward the cost of an insurance claim. The insurance company pays the rest.

3. _____ includes everything that is needed

4. _____ the money that is spent on something

5. _____ a sum of money that you pay regularly to an insurance company for an insurance policy

6. _____ actions that are intended to prevent things, such as disease

7. _____ involving surgery

C **Answer the questions about yourself.**

1. Have you ever had a surgical procedure? If so, what for? _____

2. Do you have an insurance policy that you pay a premium for? If so, how much is the premium? _____ What is the deductible? _____

3. What costs more for you every month, your auto expenditures or your medical expenditures? _____

D **Read the paragraph about Liam's family dentist, Dr. Stella. Then, answer the questions.**

Liam takes his children to a dentist, Dr. Stella, who likes to get new patients by referral. In other words, if patients like him as a dentist, they tell their friends and family about him. Hopefully, some of them will make appointments with him. Dr. Stella offers incentives for every new patient referred to him. For the first referral, he gives his patients a $20 gift card for a local coffee shop. For the second referral, he sends them an electric toothbrush, worth over $50. And every time a patient sends him a referral, Dr. Stella enters their name in a drawing to win a mountain bike. He believes that by offering his patients incentives, they will refer more people to him, thereby giving him more new clients.

1. What is a referral? _____

2. What incentives does Dr. Stella offer? _____

E **Read the definitions and example sentences of the nouns below. Then, write a sentence using each word.**

Noun	Definition	Example sentence
reduction	When something is made smaller.	Policyholders get a reduction in their deductibles if they use an approved doctor.
reimbursement	a payment to you for something you have spent money on	A medical care plan is a program that provides reimbursement for medical care expenses.
mandate	a rule or regulation	HMOs give mandates regarding what medical procedures can be used.
probability	how likely something is to happen.	A goal of HMOs is to reduce the probability of high-cost medical treatment.

1. _____

2. _____

3. _____

4. _____

F **Read the definitions. Then write an example sentence for each word.**

Noun	Definition	Example sentence
compensate	to pay someone money or give them something to replace money or things they have lost	
obtain	to get something	

G Complete the sentences with a vocabulary word in the box.

compensate	deductible	comprehensive	mandate	expenditures
incentives	obtained	premium	preventative	probability
reductions	referral	reimburse	restriction	surgical

1. Jamal has to go to the hospital for a _____ procedure.

2. Do you pay a high insurance _____ every month?

3. Will your insurance company _____ you for procedures you've already paid for?

4. My company just issued a _____ that all employees with families have to switch to HMOs.

5. Our company offers a _____ medical policy, which includes medical, dental, vision, and life insurance.

6. Does she know where free or low cost vaccinations can be _____?

7. I need to find a new dermatologist. Can you give me a _____?

8. Will your company _____ you for all the days of work you missed?

9. Most HMOs have _____ on which doctors and hospitals can be used.

10. Our medical _____ were so high last year that we considered taking out a loan.

11. Liam's insurance company offers him a _____ in medical fees if he goes to one of their approved doctors.

12. Once you meet your annual _____, your insurance company should cover the rest of your medical costs.

13. There is a high _____ that you will need to have your tooth removed.

14. The dentist encouraged them to get _____ care to make sure their gums stay healthy.

15. My doctor gives us _____ to send new patients to him.

▶ **ACADEMIC WORD LIST**

H Which words do you know?

☐ approach	☐ available	☐ benefit	☐ consists	☐ contracts
☐ financial	☐ identify	☐ individuals	☐ medical	☐ option
☐ percent	☐ policy	☐ principle	☐ procedures	☐ range
☐ requirements	☐ specific	☐ structure	☐ thereby	☐ variation

▶ DICTIONARY WORK: Parts of Speech

I Sometimes a word may have more than one part of speech. Consider the example below.

> **mandate** /mændeɪt/ (mandates, mandating, mandated) N-COUNT If someone is given a mandate to carry out a particular policy or task, they are given the official authority to do it. *Police have a mandate to protect the community.* V-T To mandate something means to make it mandatory. *The law mandates all high school students take a test in order to graduate.*

J Complete the following sentences with *mandate.* Change the form if necessary.

1. Yesterday, our boss _____ that we reread our insurance plan options before making any changes.

2. The law _____ that employees who work 40 hours must be given health insurance.

3. Their supervisor gave them a _____ to offer the best customer service possible.

K Each of the following words can be used as a noun and a verb. Look up each word and write a sentence for each, according to the definitions.

1. approach

   a. noun _____

   b. verb _____

2. benefit

   a. noun _____

   b. verb _____

3. contract

   a. noun _____

   b. verb _____

▶ PRE-READING

A Compare what you know of health care coverage in the United States to health care coverage in your native country. Think about the following questions as you complete the chart below: Who pays for health care? What types of health care coverage are offered? What types of medical services are covered?

Health Care Coverage	
United States	**Native country**
✔ medical expenses covered by employers, the government, or individuals ✔ ✔ ✔ ✔ ✔ ✔	✔ ✔ ✔ ✔ ✔ ✔ ✔ ✔ ✔

B Work with a small group to come up with the ideal medical coverage. Answer the following questions as you put your plan together.

1. Who would pay for medical expenses?
2. Where would the money come from?
3. What expenses would be covered? What expenses would not be covered?
4. What paperwork would be necessary to receive medical care?
5. How would patients choose their medical providers?

C Share your plan with the class.

► **READING**

D **Read the following excerpt from *Personal Finance,* a college textbook.**

A medical care plan is a generic[1] name for any program that pays or provides reimbursement for direct medical care expenditures. When a medical plan is available as an employee benefit, the employer typically pays the cost for the worker (and possibly other members of the worker's immediate family) for the lowest-cost plan the employer offers. Employees can choose a higher-priced option or add family members to the coverage[2] by paying an additional charge. New employees generally must make a choice among the available plans within the first few days of being hired.

Health Maintenance Organizations
Health Maintenance Organizations (HMOs) provide a broad[3] range of health care services for a set monthly fee on a prepaid basis. For the specific monthly fee, HMO members receive a wide array[4] of health care services, including hospital, surgical and preventative health care. Some HMO plans require a small copayment of $5 to $20 for each office visit or prescription. A goal of HMOs is to catch problems early, thereby reducing the probability of subsequent[5] high-cost medical treatment. HMO services are available to both groups and individuals.

The monthly fee charged by an HMO is based on the medical services that the average plan member would tend to use. HMOs do not put dollar limits on how much health care can be used. Instead they list the types of medical care they will provide under the contract. HMOs are one of several types of managed care plans. Such plans seek to control the conditions under which health care can be obtained. Examples of controls include preapproval of hospital admissions, restrictions on which hospital or doctor can be used, and mandates regarding the type of procedures that will be employed to treat a specific medical problem.

HMO subscribers[6] are assigned a primary-care physician[7] by the HMO or choose one from an approved list. The primary-care physician must order or approve referrals to specialized health care providers (for example, a cardiologist) within or outside the HMO. If the HMO itself does not provide a particular type of care, it refers the patient to a local hospital or clinic for those services. One HMO variation is the individual practice organization (IPO), a structure in which the HMO contracts with—rather than hires—groups of physicians. These physicians maintain their own offices in various locations around town and serve as the primary-care physicians and specialists[8] for the HMO.

Traditional Health Insurance
Health insurance provides protection against financial losses resulting from illness and injury. It may cover hospital, surgical, and other medical expenditures. These coverages can be purchased separately, but most consumers and employers prefer comprehensive health insurance because it combines these protections into a single policy with policy limits of $1 million or more. Unlike with HMOs, where you are prepaying for health care in advance, health insurance is based on the concept of reimbursement for losses, with the patient choosing the type of care based on the advice of his or her physician. For this reason, health insurance plans are referred to as indemnity[9] plans because they compensate the insured for the cost of care received.

[1] **generic** – describes something that refers or relates to a whole group of similar things
[2] **coverage** – a guarantee from an insurance company that money will be paid by them in particular situations
[3] **broad** – includes a large number of different things or people
[4] **array** – a large number or wide range of something
[5] **subsequent** – something that happened or existed after the time or event that has just been referred to
[6] **subscribers** – people who pay for and receive a service
[7] **primary-care physician** – the doctor you see most often for your medical needs
[8] **specialists** – doctors who specialize in certain areas of medicine
[9] **indemnity** – something that provides insurance or protection against damage or loss

Health insurance plans often identify a preferred provider organization (PPO). A PPO is a group of medical care providers (doctors, hospitals, and other health care providers) who contract with a health insurance company to provide services at a discount. This discount is then passed on along to policyholders in the form of reductions or elimination of deductibles and coinsurance requirements if they choose the PPO providers for the medical care.

Consider the case of Dru Cameron, who works for a large marketing firm in Charlotte, North Carolina. Her firm's health insurance plan has contracted with a PPO representing a local university's teaching hospital and its affiliated[10] physicians. Because Dru chose the hospital for treatment of a broken ankle, she saved $150 on the $250 deductible and did not have to pay the usual 20 percent coinsurance share of office visit charges. She gave up the right to go to her family doctor, who is not a PPO member, although she could still see that physician for other health care needs in the future.

A provider-sponsored network (PSN), also called a provider-sponsored association, is a group of cooperating physicians and hospitals who have banded together[11] to offer a health insurance contract. Such networks operate primarily in rural areas, where access to HMOs may be limited. As a group, the members of the PSN coordinate and deliver health care services and manage the insurance plan financially. They contract with outside providers for medical services that are not available through members of the group.

Consumer-Driven Health Care

Consumer-driven health care is a term describing an approach to medical care that is different than that of typical HMOs and traditional health insurance. With these two latter[12] approaches, consumers pay very little out of their own pocket for medical care and, thus, have little incentive to maximize health care spending. The principle behind consumer-driven health care is that knowledgeable and informed patients/employees will spend their own money more carefully than they would spend an employer's or health plan's funds. Therefore, consumer-driven plans require higher out-of-pocket[13] spending by consumers so that they will shop around, compare prices, pick and choose among options, and all the other things consumers normally do when making purchases.

Consumer-driven plans are based upon a high-deductible health care plan that can either be traditional health insurance or an HMO. Deductibles can start at $1,100 ($2,200 for a family) but can be as high as $5,000 per year. The plans will have an out-of-pocket limit of $5,500 for an individual or $11,000 for a family per year. High-deductible plans have lower premiums than other plans because workers pay a larger portion of health care bills. Employers like the plans for this reason. But people who must buy their own health care plan might find the lower premiums attractive as well.

The question, then, is how to afford the high out-of-pocket cost when medical care is needed. The answer is with a health savings account (HSA) or a health reimbursement account (HRA). An HSA is a tax-deductible[14] savings account into which individuals and/or their employers can deposit tax-sheltered funds[15] for use to pay medical bills including deductibles and other out-of pocket costs. The maximum annual deposit is either the annual deductible under the high-deductable plan or $2,900 for an individual or $5,800 for a family plan, whichever is lower. An HRA consists of funds set aside by employers to reimburse employees for qualified[16] medical expenses. Thus, the employer helps the employees pay their medical bills.

Source: *Personal Finance* by E. Thomas Garman and Raymond E. Forgue, 2008, pp. 301–304

---

[10] **affiliated** – officially connected to
[11] **banded together** – to join or come together
[12] **latter** – the second group of things that have been mentioned
[13] **out-of-pocket** – expenses that you pay for with your own money
[14] **tax-deductible** – an expense that can be deducted from your income tax
[15] **tax-sheltered funds** – money that has reduced taxes
[16] **qualified** – meeting the proper standards and requirements

► SKIMMING FOR DETAILS

E Decide if each statement is representative of an HMO, traditional health insurance, or consumer driven health care. Put a check (✔) in the correct column. In some cases, you will put a check (✔) in more than one column.

		HMO/IPO	Traditional (PPO, PSN)	Consumer-Driven (HSA, HRA)
1.	These plans require higher out-of-pocket spending.			
2.	Services are provided on a prepaid basis.			
3.	Patients can choose the care they want based on the advice of their physicians.			
4.	This is a managed care plan.			
5.	Services are available to groups and individuals.			
6.	These plans can involve a tax-deductible savings account.			
7.	Subscribers are assigned a primary care physician or can choose one from a list.			
8.	One type of network involved a group of physicians who work together to offer a health insurance contract.			
9.	Insurance is based on reimbursement for losses.			
10.	Policyholders will pay lower deductibles if they choose a doctor contracted with the health insurance company.			
11.	Restrictions are placed on which hospital or doctor can be used.			
12.	These plans are based on a high-deductible health care plan.			

F **Read the statements. Circle *True* or *False*.**

1. A goal of HMOs is to pay for high-cost medical treatment.	True	False
2. When a medical plan is available as an employee benefit, an employer usually pays the cost for the employee of the cheapest plan offered by the employer.	True	False
3. The monthly fee that an HMO charges is based on the medical services that an average member would use.	True	False
4. Most employers and consumers prefer to pay for hospital, surgical, and other medical expenditures separately.	True	False
5. Consumer-driven plans are always HMOs.	True	False
6. PSNs are usually found in urban areas.	True	False

G **What does each of the following abbreviations stand for?**

1. HMO: _____

2. IPO: _____

3. PPO: _____

4. PSN: _____

5. HSA: _____

6. HRA: _____

▶ **MAIN IDEAS**

H **In your own words, write one sentence explaining each of the abbreviations from above.**

1. An HMO is _____

_____

2. _____

_____

3. _____

_____

4. _____

_____

5. _____

_____

6. _____

_____

▶ READING COMPREHENSION

 Circle the best answer.

1. A medical care plan is
    a. a tax deductible savings account used to pay for medical expenses.
    b. a program that pays for direct medical care expenses.
    c. a group of doctors that work together to provide medical services.
    d. an insurance policy that reimburses patients for their out-of-pocket expenses.

2. HMOs attempt to control the conditions under which health can be obtained by
    a. restricting which doctors can be used.
    b. requiring preapproval of hospital admissions.
    c. mandating which procedures can be used for certain medical problems.
    d. all of the above.

3. Health insurance plans are referred to as indemnity plans because they
    a. pay for health care in advance.
    b. reimburse employers for insurance premiums.
    c. have a network of preferred providers.
    d. compensate the insured for the money spent on medical expenses.

4. If policyholders choose PPO providers for their medical care, they
    a. receive a discount from the provider.
    b. get a rebate from the doctor.
    c. get better advice from the doctor.
    d. get penalized by their insurance company.

5. What does the example of Dru Cameron explain?
    a. PPOs offer better medical care than HMOs.
    b. The local hospital was better than her family doctor at treating broken ankles.
    c. By going to a contracted hospital, she was able to pay a lower deductible.
    d. PPOs are cheaper than HMOs.

6. Consumer-driven health insurance assumes that
    a. consumers like to pay more for their health care.
    b. consumers will shop around for the best price.
    c. consumers can't afford an HMO or PPO.
    d. consumers have a lot of savings to pay for medical expenses.

▶ WRITING CHALLENGE: Compare and Contrast

A A compare and contrast paragraph is a piece of writing that describes the similarities and differences between two things.
Read the compare and contrast paragraph that Blanca wrote.

> *Different Health Care Plans*
>
> My husband Matthew and I both work for companies that offer health care plans to their full-time employees. The plans offered to us have some similarities and many differences. First of all, my company offers more choices. Matthew's company offers HMO coverage. Similarly, my company offers HMO coverage. However, it also offers PPO coverage. Second, Matthew must go to the doctor assigned to him. In contrast, under the PPO program that I chose, I can see any doctor I want. Third, we both have co-pays for our medical care, but Matthew's is lower. He pays $5 every time he sees the doctor, while I have to pay $20 every time I see the doctor. Although I'd rather have a lower co-pay, it's more important to me to be able to choose my doctor. All in all, I prefer the health care plan offered to me by my company rather than the one offered to my husband.

B Answer the following questions.

1. What is the paragraph comparing and contrasting? _____

   _____

2. What are the similarities? _____

   _____

3. What are the differences? _____

   _____

4. Which health care plan does Blanca like better? Why? _____

   _____

▶ CHOOSE A TOPIC

C Choose one of the following topics for your compare and contrast paragraph. Circle the topic you choose.

1. Compare and contrast the health care plans offered in your native country to those offered in the United States.
2. Compare and contrast your health care plan to the health care plan of someone you know.

► BRAINSTORM: Outline Your Paragraph

D **Look at the outline of Blanca's paragraph. Fill in the blanks with supporting details from her paragraph.**

TOPIC SENTENCE: <u>My husband Matthew and I both work for companies that offer health care plans to their full-time employees. The plans offered to us have some similarities and many differences.</u>

1. Health care choices

    a. _____

    b. _____

2. Choice of doctor

    a. _____

    b. _____

3. Co-pays

    a. _____

    b. _____

CONCLUSION SENTENCE: <u>All in all, I prefer the health care plan offered to me by my company than the one offered to my husband.</u>

E **Think of three main points you could compare and contrast in your paragraph. For ideas, look at the Health Care Coverage chart you filled out on page 70 and recall what you learned from the reading.**

EXAMPLE: <u>cost, who pays for it, choice of doctors</u>

1. _____

2. _____

3. _____

F **What two details do you have to support each main point? Write short notes below.**

Point 1: _____ _____

_____

Point 2: _____ _____

_____

Point 3: _____ _____

_____

G   **Using your notes from Exercise F, write an outline for your paragraph.**

TOPIC SENTENCE: _____

_____

1. _____
   a. _____
   b. _____

2. _____
   a. _____
   b. _____

3. _____
   a. _____
   b. _____

CONCLUSION SENTENCE: _____

_____

► TRANSITIONS

H   **Look back at Blanca's paragraph and underline the transitions used to connect ideas.**

Introduce an Idea	Compare	Contrast
First	Likewise	However
Second	Similarly	In contrast
Third	In a similar manner	Although
Finally	In the same way	Even though
All in all	Also	On the other hand

Which transitions will you use in your paragraph? Circle at least six from above.

► VOCABULARY

I   **Look back at the new words you learned in this unit from the vocabulary pages and from the Academic Word List. Which words do you think might fit into your paragraph? Make a list of at least six words below.**

1. _____   4. _____

2. _____   5. _____

3. _____   6. _____

▶ WRITE A ROUGH DRAFT

J Using the ideas you have outlined, write your paragraph on a separate piece of paper. Do not forget to connect your ideas with transitions and include some new vocabulary words.

▶ EDIT THE ROUGH DRAFT: Content

K Look back at your paragraph and answer the following questions.

1. Is my paragraph clearly written and easy to understand? _____
2. Did I give my paragraph a title? _____
3. Did I include a topic sentence? _____
4. Did I include a conclusion sentence? _____
5. Did I include two supporting details for each topic? _____
6. Did I connect my ideas with transitions? _____
7. Did I include some of the new vocabulary words? _____ How many? _____
8. How could I make my paragraph better? _____
   _____

L Read your paragraph again and make changes based on the questions you answered above.

▶ EDIT THE ROUGH DRAFT: Mechanics

M Use the chart below to edit the mechanics of your paragraph.

✔ EDITING CHECKLIST

	Yes	No
The first word of my title is capitalized.	☐	☐
Every word in my title is capitalized (except for small words: a, an, the, in, etc.).	☐	☐
The first letter of every sentence is capitalized.	☐	☐
Every sentence ends with a punctuation mark.	☐	☐
Every sentence has a subject and a verb.	☐	☐
The subject and the verb agree in every sentence.	☐	☐
All of the words are spelled correctly.	☐	☐

N Now go back and make the mechanical changes to your story.

▶ PEER EDITING

O Exchange your paragraph with a partner. Have your partner read your paragraph and use the same checklist to help you make mechanical changes to your story

P Have your partner answer the following questions about your paragraph.

1. Is the paragraph clear and easy to understand?
2. Did the author include a title?
3. Did the author include a topic sentence that explains what the paragraph will be about?
4. Did the author include at least three main points?
5. Did the author add some supporting details to better explain each main point?
6. Did the author use transitions to connect the main points?
7. Did the author use some new vocabulary words?
8. Did the author end with a conclusion sentence?
9. How could the paragraph be better?

Q Talk to your partner about your paragraph. Go back and make any changes that you think will improve your story.

▶ WRITE THE FINAL PAPER

R Write your final paper. Remember the following formatting tips as you write.

1. Put the title at the top center of your paper.
2. Put a space between the title and the first paragraph.
3. Indent the first word of every paragraph.
4. Make sure there are left and right margins on your paper.
5. Write neatly.

S Proof your final paper.

▶ Community Challenge

Research different health insurance plans available to you and your family.

UNIT 6 — Retail

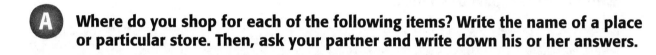

▶ GETTING READY

A Where do you shop for each of the following items? Write the name of a place or particular store. Then, ask your partner and write down his or her answers.

Retail item	Places I shop	Places my partner shops
shoes		
clothing		
books		
music		
tools		
fruits and vegetables		
toilet paper		
electronics		

B In a small group, discuss the following questions.

1. Do you look for sales when you shop or do you shop at the most convenient places?

2. Do you take a shopping list with you?

3. Do you sometimes buy things that weren't on your list? If so, what sort of things?

4. How often do you return things you've bought? For what reasons?

5. What is more important to you, price or quality?

6. Do you try to support small businesses or do you prefer to shop at the larger chain stores? Why?

► VOCABULARY CHALLENGE

A Look at the words. Check (✔) the words that you know.

☐ accessibility   ☐ accountability   ☐ advocates   ☐ awareness   ☐ consult

☐ decline   ☐ derives   ☐ destruction   ☐ evidence   ☐ expand

☐ gradual   ☐ implement   ☐ legitimate   ☐ preserve   ☐ source

B The words have been grouped below according to their parts of speech. Some words appear in more than one column. Read each list and label each column with the correct part of speech.

Parts of Speech		
1.	**2.**	**3.**
accessibility decline accountability advocates destruction awareness evidence source	decline derives implemented advocates preserve consult expand source	gradual legitimate

C Circle the correct word in each sentence based on its part of speech.

1. For years, environmentalists, farmers, and small-business _legitimate / advocates_ have been trying to convince people to buy locally grown food.

2. National companies such as grocer Whole Foods and food-supplier SYSCO have recently announced plans to _source / gradual_ much more of their produce locally.

3. A growing _awareness / preserve_ of two separate but related issues—organic standards and fossil fuels—has made the local-food discussion more urgent.

4. The organic-food industry has _destruction / expanded_ from small farmers to corporate producers.

5. Some critics have grown concerned that the organic-certification standards _implemented / accountability_ by the USDA in 2002 won't last.

6. Alongside _decline / legitimate_ questions about _accessibility / consult_ is the cultural impression that all food should be cheap, regardless of how it is made and how far it travels.

D **Replace each italicized word or phrase with a word from the box.**

accountability	consulted	declines	derives
destruction	evidence	gradual	preserve

1. Transporting food from far-away can cause environmental _____ (ruin).

2. There is _____ (proof) that local food is moving increasingly into the mainstream.

3. Culture doesn't change right away. It's _____ (slowly over time).

4. Gabriela has been interested in local and organic food since college, when she _____ (got advice from) a nutritionist.

5. There is a theory that global petroleum production will soon reach a peak and then rapidly _____ (decrease).

6. Many feel that small farmers are more likely to _____ (protect) soil and water quality than corporate growers are.

7. Irani _____ (gets) joy from her relationships with farmers.

8. Having to face their customers at farmer's markets holds them to a high level of _____ (responsibility).

E **Match each word to its definition.**

_____ 1. accessibility   a. the act of noticing or realizing something

_____ 2. accountability   b. deterioration or reduction

_____ 3. advocates   c. ask for advice

_____ 4. awareness   d. the process of destroying or ruining

_____ 5. consult   e. make or become larger

_____ 6. decline   f. availability

_____ 7. derives   g. happening slowly

_____ 8. destruction   h. reasonable and justified

_____ 9. evidence   i. maintain something

_____ 10. expand   j. people who give support

_____ 11. gradual   k. locate something for use

_____ 12. implement   l. sign or proof

_____ 13. legitimate   m. responsibility

_____ 14. preserve   n. carry out or fulfill something

_____ 15. source   o. get something

F **Look at the following sentences with *italicized* expressions. What do you think each expression means? Complete the chart by writing your own definitions. Use your dictionary if you need to.**

1. The only thing I can make *from scratch* is banana bread.

2. She is always *beating the local drum* by telling her friends how delicious the vegetables are at the local farmers' market.

3. Restaurants in San Francisco *pay homage* to local farmers by creating recipes with their produce.

4. Although it is *time-consuming* to shop around for the freshest fruit, the taste makes it all worth it.

5. It gives many people *peace of mind* to know exactly where their meat has come from.

6. She *muddles through* the newspaper every week just to find the best deals and clip coupons.

7. His decision to buy in bulk at a big chain store was *tied to* price, not quality.

Expression	Definition
from scratch	
beating the local drum	
pay homage	
time-consuming	
peace of mind	
muddle through	
tied to	

► ACADEMIC WORD LIST

G Which words do you know?

- ☐ commitment
- ☐ commodity
- ☐ considerable
- ☐ consists
- ☐ conventionally
- ☐ convince
- ☐ corporate
- ☐ global
- ☐ institute
- ☐ issues
- ☐ logical
- ☐ policy
- ☐ relying
- ☐ researcher
- ☐ sustenance
- ☐ theory
- ☐ traditions
- ☐ transport
- ☐ version
- ☐ culture

► DICTIONARY WORK: Parts of Speech

H Look up each of the following words and write their parts of speech. (*Note:* Some words may have more than one part of speech. If so, write all of them.) If the dictionary has a sample sentence, write it. If not, write your own example sentence using the word.

1. **conventionally**   Part of speech: _____

Example sentence: _____

2. **harvest**   Part of speech: _____

Example sentence: _____

3. **organic**   Part of speech: _____

Example sentence: _____

4. **commodity**   Part of speech: _____

Example sentence: _____

5. **pervasive**   Part of speech: _____

Example sentence: _____

6. **sustenance**   Part of speech: _____

Example sentence: _____

7. **industrialized**   Part of speech: _____

Example sentence: _____

8. **consist**   Part of speech: _____

Example sentence: _____

9. **devastated**   Part(s) of speech: _____

Example sentence: _____

10. **policy**   Part(s) of speech: _____

Example sentence: _____

▶ PRE-READING

A **A carnivore only eats meat. An herbivore only eats plants. What do you think a *locavore* eats?**

_____

B **The 100-Mile Diet is an eating plan in which dieters, better known as "locavores," try to eat only, or mostly, food grown within 100 miles of their homes. Answer the following questions about your own eating habits.**

1. Do you eat any foods that are locally grown? If so, what? _____

   _____

2. Where do you get this locally grown food? _____

   _____

3. How much of your food do you buy at the grocery store? _____

4. Does your grocery store sell any locally grown food? _____

5. Do you think locally grown food is cheaper or more expensive? Why or why not?

   _____

   _____

C **Read each of the following quotes. Do you agree or disagree?**

1. "Produce bought directly from local farmers is actually the best hope for fresh, healthy food."

   _____ agree   _____ disagree

2. "Milk is milk, eggs are eggs, and meat is meat . . . it's all the same."

   _____ agree   _____ disagree

3. "Most people will happily spend several dollars on a bag of potato chips that has maybe a few potatoes in it and almost no nutritional value. But they'll scoff at a five-pound bag of local organic potatoes for the same price."

   _____ agree   _____ disagree

4. "If you're too busy to feed your family well, maybe you need to re-examine your priorities."

   _____ agree   _____ disagree

D **Discuss your answers with a partner. Why do you agree or disagree?**

► **READING**

Twilight Greenway is a freelance writer from San Francisco who produces the website/e-letter for the Center for Urban Education about Sustainable Agriculture (CUESA) in San Francisco. Read the article she wrote for *Culinate*, a website engaged in the ongoing conversation about learning to eat well.

Going Local: "Locavores" Redefine Where Food Should Come From

By Twilight Greenaway

January 29, 2007

On a cold November Saturday, Anita Prammer, 22, travels across town to a small parking lot to pick up some bread. This late in the year, all of the outdoor farmers' markets in Minneapolis have shut down; the local growing season has essentially come to a close. Prammer is one of more than 60 customers who have ordered bread from a baker who uses locally produced ingredients.

The baker, Brett Laidlaw, has set up in the parking lot with a few other vendors selling local meat, honey, pickles, and late-season apples. He recognizes Prammer, hands over her order, and chats[1] about the next time he'll have bread available, right before the winter holidays.

Prammer came to Minneapolis in September to intern[2] at the Institute for Agriculture[3] and Trade Policy. She started buying the bulk[4] of her food directly from local farmers around the same time. She'd read about the 100-Mile Diet, an eating plan in which the dieters, better known as "locavores," try to eat only, or mostly, food grown within 100 miles of their homes. Throughout the fall, she says, 80 to 90 percent of her diet was produced in Minnesota.

Environmentalists, farmers, and small-business advocates have been beating the local drum for decades. But in recent years, the idea of supporting local food has traveled from fringe[5] to mainstream. Between 1994 and 2004, the number of farmers' markets in the U.S. more than doubled. Restaurants across the country pay homage to the local products behind their menus. And national companies such as grocer Whole Foods and food-supplier SYSCO have recently touted[6] plans to source much more of their produce locally.

The phrase "100-Mile Diet" is most commonly associated with Alisa Smith and James MacKinnon, two writers who kept an exceptionally detailed account of their attempt to eat locally in British Columbia for an entire year. But their project is only one example of a variety of challenges and diets to choose from. Some locavores try eating locally because they wish to support local farmers; others, because they believe in the health benefits of local food; still others, because they feel that eating locally is a powerful political, economic, and environmental statement.

A growing awareness of two separate but related issues—organic standards and fossil fuels[7]—has made the local-food discussion more urgent. As the organic-food industry has expanded from small farmers to corporate producers, some critics have grown concerned that the organic-certification standards implemented by the USDA in 2002 won't last. Many feel that small farmers are more likely to preserve soil and water quality than corporate growers, and many small farmers agree, refusing organic certification (an expensive, time-consuming process anyway) in favor of

[1] **chats** – talk informally
[2] **intern** – work as a trainee
[3] **agriculture** – farming
[4] **bulk** – majority
[5] **fringe** – edge, outer limit
[6] **touted** – praised
[7] **fossil fuels** –fuels derived from prehistoric organisms

farming practices they believe are better environmentally. Meanwhile, petroleum products are pervasive[8] in every step of the industrialized[9] farming process. They're used to make fertilizers,[10] herbicides,[11] and pesticides.[12] They're used to make and power the machinery that tills[13] the soil and harvests the produce. And they're essential[14] for the trucks and trains that transport most of the food sold in the U.S.

In Albany, New York, the fossil-fuel problem swayed[15] molecular biologist[16] Cheryl Nechamen. Like Prammer, she became a locavore in September. But while Prammer's choice to go local was tied more to organics, Nechamen's decision was due to her discovery of "peak oil," the theory that global petroleum[17] production will soon reach a peak[18] and then rapidly decline. According to the Worldwatch Institute, an independent research organization that studies environmental and social issues, most food in the U.S. travels 1,500 to 2,500 miles to get from farm to table, and requires as much as 10 percent of the nation's oil spending. So for Nechamen, the choice to stop buying conventionally grown food was clear.

"We can muddle through with the other problems we'll have when peak oil arrives—getting to work, keeping our houses warm, keeping the lights on—but we can't tell people to wait a few months to eat while we change our whole agricultural system," she says.

In northern Maryland, Sarah Irani organized a version of the challenge that involved hosting farmer talks and a local-food potluck. "I've found that the most powerful thing has been changing my own life," says the 29-year-old artist and teacher. "People come over for dinner, or I talk to them at church. And you don't really feel the effect right away, but that's kind of how culture changes. It's *gradual*."

Irani has been interested in local and organic food since college, when she consulted a naturopath[19] for medical problems. Her diet today, she says, consists of 70 to 80 percent local foods. "Every now and again, I'll buy some bananas, or I'll use some Indian spices to cook with," she admits. "I'm not going to be totally hardnosed[20] about it, because trade has brought some really great things." People who set themselves up to eat only local foods all the time, she worries, are much less likely to succeed over the long term.

Like Prammer, Irani derives sustenance not just from the food she eats but from the relationships she creates. When she found a bad egg in a local dozen recently, she called the farmer—whom she knows well—and told him. He was devastated, she says, and offered a replacement. But for Irani, it was the peace of mind that really mattered.

For Jessica Prentice, the co-founder of the Bay Area's Eat Local Challenge, that kind of interaction is exactly what drives[21] the local food movement. Knowing your local farmers means you can ask them direct questions: How do you treat your soil? What do you feed your cows? "It holds them to a level of accountability that's far beyond what an organic certification does," says Prentice.

Of course, accountability doesn't come cheap. Eating locally also generally means spending more. Marc Rumminger says his food expenditures were higher than normal during the month-long

---

[8] **pervasive** – something that is present or felt throughout a place or thing
[9] **industrialized** – developed, modern
[10] **fertilizers** – substance aiding plant growth
[11] **herbicides** – chemical substance for killing unwanted plants
[12] **pesticides** – chemical substance for killing pests
[13] **tills** –turn over, plow, cultivate
[14] **essential** – necessary
[15] **swayed** – influenced
[16] **molecular biologist** – someone who studies the science of molecules
[17] **petroleum** – crude oil found in rock
[18] **peak** – maximum quantity
[19] **naturopath** – professional who specializes in drug-free medical treatment
[20] **hardnosed** – uncompromising
[21] **drives** – steer progress of something

Bay Area challenge but, he says, "this is a place where I want my money to go. So I think that was an important part of it: *the idea of letting my personal market spaces do something useful.*"

Brian Halweil, a senior researcher at the Worldwatch Institute and the author of *Eat Here: Reclaiming Homegrown Pleasures in a Global Supermarket,* understands why local food is popular with what he refers to as the "culinary elite,[22]" but says he also sees evidence that it is moving increasingly into the mainstream.

A number of multinational corporations,[23] Halweil points out, are beginning to see local food programs as a logical next step in greening[24] their public images. In addition to Whole Foods, Wal-Mart recently launched[25] a pilot[26] local-food buying program called "Salute to America's Farmer." When the program launched in September, the Wal-Mart website announced that "local farmers and growers in all 50 states will be spotlighted[27] throughout the upcoming year."

Halweil also points out that in many of the poorest urban neighborhoods, where liquor and convenience stores far outnumber grocery stores, farmers' markets are filling the produce gap. In such neighborhoods—he cites Anacostia, one of the poorest areas of Washington, D.C.—"produce bought directly from local farmers is actually the best hope for fresh, healthy food."

Alongside legitimate questions about accessibility, says Prentice, is the cultural impression that all food should be cheap, regardless of how it is made and how far it travels. "There's been a huge campaign to convince the American people that, by and large, milk is milk, eggs are eggs, and meat is meat ... it's all the same," she says. "It doesn't matter how the animals were treated, what they ate." Before industrial agriculture, she argues, "most people understood that there were all these subtleties[28] in our food system." Local food, she says, is simply food with an honest price tag, without the hidden costs of transport, environmental destruction, and the loss of small independent farms.

Halweil agrees. A considerable barrier,[29] he says, that keeps people of all class backgrounds from eating local foods is the habit of relying on convenience foods over fresh foods. "Most people will happily spend several dollars on a bag of potato chips that has maybe a few potatoes in it and almost no nutritional value," Halweil says. "But they'll scoff[30] at a five-pound bag of local organic potatoes for the same price."

Of course, cooking everything from scratch takes time, another commodity[31] demanded of those participating in local food challenges. Sarah Irani says she and her husband ate a lot of venison[32] and rutabagas[33] last winter, but the experience made her want to learn to prepare for the Maryland seasons the old-fashioned way.

When Irani talks about her commitment to local food, she paraphrases Sally Fallon, author of the book *Nourishing Traditions*. "Sallen says, yes, it takes time," she says. "But if you're too busy to feed your family well, maybe you need to re-examine your priorities."

[22] **culinary elite** – people, including chefs, who take food very seriously
[23] **multinational corporations** – companies that operate in several countries
[24] **greening** – increasing environmental awareness and taking action
[25] **launched** – start a program
[26] **pilot** – trial run of something
[27] **spotlighted** –focused attention on something
[28] **subtleties** – fine distinctions
[29] **barrier** – something that obstructs or limits
[30] **scoff** – make fun of
[31] **commodity** – useful thing
[32] **venison** – deer meat
[33] **rutabagas** – root turnips

▶ SKIMMING FOR DETAILS

F **There are many people mentioned in the article. Match each person to his or her description.**

_____ 1. Sarah Irani

_____ 2. Anita Prammer

_____ 3. Cheryl Nechamen

_____ 4. Sally Fallon

_____ 5. Marc Rumminger

_____ 6. Alisa Smith and James MacKinnon

_____ 7. Brian Halweil

_____ 8. Jessica Prentice

a. two writers who kept an account of their attempt to eat locally for a year, known as the "100-Mile Diet"

b. participated in the Bay Area Challenge

c. Maryland resident who hosts farmer talks

d. intern at the Institute for Agriculture and Trade

e. co-founder of Bay Area's Eat Local Challenge

f. molecular biologist

g. author of *Nourishing Traditions*

h. researcher at Worldwatch Institute

▶ MAIN IDEAS

G **Each of the people above contributes a main idea to the article. Read each main idea below and write the name of the person who contributed it.**

1. Buy local so you can support local farmers. <u>Alisa Smith and James MacKinnon</u>

2. There is evidence that local food is moving into the mainstream.

   _____

3. Participation in eating locally will change your life.

   _____

4. Eating locally means spending more money on food.

   _____

5. Feeding your family well should be a priority.

   _____

6. Buy local so you can eat organic food.

   _____

7. The local food movement is being driven by the relationships between farmers and customers.

   _____

8. Eating locally can help decrease our need for petroleum.

   _____

▶ READING COMPREHENSION

H **Discuss the following questions with a small group. When you come up with an answer that you all agree on, write it on the lines.**

1. What caused Anita Prammer to start buying food from local farmers? _____
   _____

2. Which three groups of people have been "beating the local drum"? _____
   _____

3. Now that you've seen the phrase in context, what does "beating the local drum" mean in this article? _____
   _____

4. In recent years, what evidence has there been that supporting local food has moved into the mainstream? _____
   _____
   _____

5. What are three reasons that locavores eat locally grown food? _____
   _____
   _____

6. Where did the phrase "100-Mile Diet" come from? _____
   _____

7. Why are some small farmers refusing organic certification? _____
   _____
   _____

8. What are petroleum products used for? _____
   _____

9. What would happen if we ran out of petroleum? _____
   _____

10. What does Jessica Prentice say makes farmers accountable? _____
    _____
    _____

11. According to Brian Halweil, what evidence is there that local food is moving into the mainstream? _____
    _____
    _____

12. What keeps people from eating local foods? _____
13. What did you learn from this article? _____
    _____
    _____

► WRITING CHALLENGE: Cause and Effect

A A *cause* is a reason something happens. It usually answers the question, "Why?" An *effect* is what happens as the result of the cause. It usually answers the question, "What?" Look at the statement below.

More people are starting to buy locally grown food because there are more farmers' markets.

- The cause is: There are more farmers' markets.
- The effect is: More people are starting to buy locally grown food.

B List other causes that explain why more people are starting to buy locally grown food.

1. _____
2. _____
3. _____
4. _____

Now, list details that support the causes you came up with.

1. _____
2. _____
3. _____
4. _____

C Read the cause and effect paragraph that Amy wrote. Then, answer the questions on the next page.

> Recently, I've noticed that my local supermarket is starting to carry more local and organic food. I believe they've changed their fresh produce offering for three reasons. First of all, they've been losing customers to farmers' markets. As a result, they have started stocking their shelves with some of the same items the farmers sell. Second of all, there has been a lot of publicity lately about the health effects of organic food. Therefore, the supermarkets want to offer a better selection of what people need to eat in order to stay healthy. Finally, I think my supermarket wants to compete with other supermarkets in the area. Since all of them are not offering local and organic produce yet, my market wants to attract the customers who want those items. Whatever the reasons, I'm happy to be shopping at a place that sells the healthy food I want to eat.

1. The effect in this paragraph is that Amy's local supermarket is starting to carry more local and organic food. What are the causes?

   a. _____

   b. _____

   c. _____

2. What details does Amy provide for each cause?

   a. _____

   b. _____

   c. _____

▶ CHOOSE A TOPIC

D **Choose one of the effects below as a topic for your paragraph.**

1. More farmers' markets are popping up across the nation.
2. More people are starting to buy locally grown food.
3. Corporations are starting to support local food.

▶ BRAINSTORM

E **Go back to the brainstorming you did on the previous page or brainstorm new ideas for your paragraph. Think of at least three main points for your topic. Then, come up with at least one supporting detail for each main point.**

Topic:		
Main point:	Main point:	Main point:
Detail:	Detail:	Detail:

F **Using your ideas from Exercise E, write an outline for your paragraph.**

TOPIC SENTENCE: _____

_____

1. _____

    a. _____

    b. _____

2. _____

    a. _____

    b. _____

3. _____

    a. _____

    b. _____

CONCLUSION SENTENCE: _____

_____

► TRANSITIONS

G **Consider the transitions used for causes and effect.**

Effects	Causes
Therefore,	(effect) . . . due to . . . (cause)
Consequently,	(effect) . . . because of . . . (cause)
As a result,	(effect) . . . because . . . (cause)
For this reason	(effect) . . . because of . . . (cause)

EXAMPLE: (cause)

There have been many recent news stories about the harmful effects of pesticides.

              (effect)

As a result, people have started buying and eating more organic food.

    (effect)   (cause)

People eating organically could be **due to** the recent health scares regarding pesticides on food.

H **Choose one of the ideas from your outline and write it using transitions. Write it two different ways.**

1. _____

_____

2. _____

_____

▶ VOCABULARY

I Look back at the new words you learned in this unit from the vocabulary pages and from the Academic Word List. What words do you think might fit into your paragraph? Make a list of at least six words below.

1. _____   4. _____
2. _____   5. _____
3. _____   6. _____

▶ WRITE A ROUGH DRAFT

J Using ideas you have outlined, write your paragraph on a separate piece of paper. Do not forget to connect your ideas with transitions and include some new vocabulary words.

▶ EDIT THE ROUGH DRAFT: Content

K Look back at your paragraph and answer the following questions.

1. Is my paragraph clearly written and easy to understand? _____
2. Did I give my paragraph a title? _____
3. Did I include a topic sentence? _____
4. Did I include a conclusion sentence? _____
5. Did I include two supporting details for each main point? _____
6. Did I connect my ideas with transitions? _____
7. Did I include some of the new vocabulary words? _____ How many? _____
8. How could I make my paragraph better? _____
   _____

L Read your paragraph again and make any changes based on the questions you answered above.

▶ EDIT THE ROUGH DRAFT: Mechanics

M Answer the questions below to edit the mechanics of your paragraph.

1. Is the first word of my title capitalized? Is every word in my title capitalized (except for small words like a, an, the, in, etc.)?
2. Is the first letter of every sentence capitalized?
3. Does every sentence end with a punctuation mark?
4. Does every sentence have a subject and a verb?
5. In every sentence, do the subject and the verb agree?
6. Are all the words in the correct order?
7. Are all of the words spelled correctly?

N Now go back and make the mechanical changes to your story.

► PEER EDITING

O Now, exchange your paragraph with a partner. Have your partner read your paragraph and answer the same questions to help you make mechanical changes to your story.

P Have your partner answer the following questions about your paragraph.

1. Is the paragraph clear and easy to understand?
2. Did the author include a title?
3. Did the author include a topic sentence that explains what the paragraph will be about?
4. Did the author include at least three main points?
5. Did the author add some supporting details to better explain each main point?
6. Did the author use transitions to connect the main points?
7. Did the author use some new vocabulary words?
8. Did the author end with a conclusion sentence?
9. How could the paragraph be better?

Q Talk to your partner about your paragraph and go back and make any changes that you think will improve your story.

► WRITE THE FINAL PAPER

R Write your final paper. Remember the following formatting tips as you write.

1. Put the title at the top center of your paper.
2. Put a space between the title and the first paragraph.
3. Indent the first word of every paragraph.
4. Make sure there are left and right margins on your paper.
5. Write neatly.

S Proof your final paper.

► Community Challenge

T Research locally grown food in your community.

1. Find at least three farmers' markets.
2. Find out what locally grown or organic foods your supermarket carries.

UNIT 7

The Office

A Look at the jobs you might find in an office. Discuss each job with a small group and write a brief description of what you think each person does.

Office Job	Job Description
accountant	
administrative assistant	
chief executive officer (CEO)	
computer technician	
customer service representative	
human resources administrator	
marketing executive	
Web designer	

B Rank the jobs in each category listed in the chart (1 being the best or highest, and 10 being the worst or lowest).

Office Job	Most Education Required	Most Experience Required	Highest Pay	Best Job
accountant				
administrative assistant				
chief executive officer (CEO)				
computer technician				
customer service representative				
human resources administrator				
marketing executive				
Web designer				

A Look at the words. Check (✔) the words that you know.

☐ compels ☐ compensate ☐ contribution ☐ desire ☐ entice

☐ excel ☐ exemplary ☐ intrigued ☐ motivation ☐ resisted

☐ revenue ☐ reward ☐ subjective ☐ thorough ☐ visibly

B Read each sentence below and decide what part of speech the italicized words are. Then, write each word in the correct column in the chart below.

1. How do you *reward* an employee for work that goes above and beyond what he or she is supposed to do?
2. What *contribution* have you made to your team?
3. How do you properly *compensate* an employee for a great idea?
4. Some employees would rather have a cash *bonus* than more vacation days.
5. One programmer's idea translated *visibly* and directly into a lot of money.
6. Here is a question that has long *intrigued* me: How do you pay employees based on performance when performance is so hard to quantify?
7. Your intrinsic motivation *compels* you to do a *thorough* job.
8. Most people start out with the *desire* to *excel* at whatever they do.
9. In the workplace, judging performance is a *subjective* exercise.
10. She was an *exemplary* employee and we were sad to lose her.
11. We hoped the offer of more stock would *entice* him to come back and work for us.

Parts of Speech			
Noun	**Verb**	**Adjective**	**Adverb**

C Match the meaning of each word below based on the context of the word in the sentences from Exercise B.

_____ 1. bonus

_____ 2. compel

_____ 3. compensate

_____ 4. contribution

_____ 5. desire

_____ 6. entice

_____ 7. excel

_____ 8. exemplary

_____ 9. intrigued

_____ 10. reward

_____ 11. subjective

_____ 12. thorough

_____ 13. visibly

a. to persuade someone to do something
b. to be very good at something
c. based on personal opinions rather than facts
d. pay someone for something they have done
e. to give someone something beneficial as a result of something they have done
f. a strong wish to do or have something
g. done carefully, in a detailed way
h. extra money
i. to be interested and want to know more about something
j. able to be seen
k. something you do to help something or someone succeed
l. extremely good
m. force someone to do something

D Revenue is money that a company, organization, or government receives from people. How do the following companies or organizations receive revenue?

1. grocery store _____

2. school _____

3. car wash _____

4. airline _____

5. amusement park _____

E Your motivation for doing something is what causes you to want to do it. What is your motivation for going to school?

_____

_____

F Read each expression and the example sentences. What do you think each expression means? Come up with your own definition and write in the table.

Expression	Definition + Sentences
the nature of	**Definition:** Nathan is shy but he has to talk to a lot of people every day. He's a customer service representative, so that's *the nature of* his job. *The nature of* our business is keeping up with the trends of teenagers.
conditional on	**Definition:** Her bonus was *conditional on* her reaching a certain amount of sales for the year. Getting benefits is *conditional on* you making it through your probation period.
bound to	**Definition:** Employees are always *bound to* think they deserve more money. He's *bound to* look for another job if we don't reward him or his efforts.
in place	**Definition:** Their company had a system *in place* for reordering supplies when they got low. He put controls *in place* for making sure the employees were recognized for their contributions to the company.

G Complete each sentence with an expression from above.

1. She is _____ get a raise if she keeps up all that hard work.

2. It's _____ her job to sit behind a computer all day.

3. We have a great training program _____ to help new employees learn the ropes.

4. Their success is _____ people purchasing their stock.

▶ **ACADEMIC WORD LIST**

H Which words do you know?

☐ accurately   ☐ assigning   ☐ bond   ☐ community   ☐ consequences

☐ consumers   ☐ depressed   ☐ displacing   ☐ draft   ☐ dramatic

☐ environment   ☐ establish   ☐ interactions   ☐ obviously   ☐ precisely

☐ project   ☐ psychologists   ☐ publish   ☐ site   ☐ solely

I There are many verbs that are paired with a preposition when used in a sentence. Oftentimes you can find these pairings in your dictionary. Consider the following example:

> **excel** /ɪksɛl/ (excels, excelling, excelled) V If someone **excels in** something or **excels at** it, they are good at doing it. *Mary excelled at outdoor sports.*

What are the two different verb + preposition pairings noted in the definition?

excel _____   excel _____

J Use your dictionary to find the prepositions that go with each verb. If your dictionary has an example sentence, write it below. If not, write your own.

1. compel _____

Sentence: _____

2. compensate _____

Sentence: _____

3. rely _____

Sentence: _____

4. derive _____

Sentence: _____

5. provide _____

Sentence: _____

6. bound _____   bound _____

Sentence: _____

Sentence: _____

▶ PRE-READING

A Read the introduction to the magazine article you are about to read. What do you think the article will be about?

> A young employee came up with an idea that added a million dollars to our bottom line. How do we reward him for the contribution? Do we even have to?

B Read each of the following ideas from the article. Do you agree or disagree?

1. The minute you start giving bonuses to reward performance, people start to compare themselves with their co-workers.

   _____ agree   _____ disagree

2. You shouldn't pay an employee extra for doing what he was hired to do.

   _____ agree   _____ disagree

3. Rewarding workers for a job well done tends to make them think they are doing it only for the reward; if the reward stops, the good work stops.

   _____ agree   _____ disagree

4. Human beings, by their nature, tend to think of themselves as a bit more wonderful than they really are.

   _____ agree   _____ disagree

C Discuss the above ideas with a partner. Why do you agree or disagree?

D Discuss the following questions with a small group. Come up with some ideas to share with your class.

1. How do you properly compensate an employee for a great idea?
2. How do you pay employees based on performance when performance is so hard to quantify?

Joel Spolsky is the co-founder and CEO of Fog Creek Software and the host of the popular blog Joel on Software. Read the column he wrote for *Inc. Magazine*.

How Hard Could It Be?: Thanks or No Thanks

A young employee came up with an idea that added a million dollars to our bottom line.[1] How do we reward him for the contribution? Do we even have to?

BY JOEL SPOLSKY

Two years ago, Noah Weiss, a young programmer who spent the summer working here at Fog Creek Software, came to me with a business idea. Noah, who was still in college, had noticed that a lot of smaller tech-related blogs were running classified ads for job listings. He suggested that we do the same thing on my company's blog, Joel on Software. The site is read by thousands of programmers a month—the ones who are so good at programming they have spare time[2] at work to read the self-absorbed drivel[3] I publish there.

Building an online classified ad system would be easy, Noah argued. (As any programmer would tell you: "It's one table!") And Fog Creek already had systems in place for charging credit cards, printing receipts, and accepting purchase orders, so the whole project wouldn't take much work.

At first, I *resisted*. I had never run ads of any sort on the site and liked the idea of keeping it commercial-free.

But Noah kept arguing. "These 37signals guys are getting 50 ads a month," he said, referring to a well-known[4] software company in Chicago. "At $250 each, that's—"

Wait, I interrupted. They charge $250 for each ad? I had imagined that the going price to run a job listing would be, oh, I don't know, $4?

That's right, Noah said. They charge $250 per ad. "Besides," he went on, "a job listing is not really an ad—it's providing a community service."

By then I had almost stopped listening. Little gears were turning in my head[5]: $250 times 50 ads times 12 months—that revenue would allow me to hire another programmer! So we added classified ads to the site. Noah wrote the first draft of the code[6] in about two weeks, and I spent another two weeks polishing[7] and debugging[8] it. The total time to build the job listing service was roughly a month.

Instead of charging the going rate of $250, we decided to charge $350. Why not? I figured we could establish ourselves as having the premium product simply by charging a premium. In the absence of additional information, consumers often use prices to judge products, and I wanted our site to be the Lexus of job listings. A few months later, 37signals raised its price to $300.

By the time you read this, that little four-week project will have made Fog Creek Software $1 million—nearly all of it profit. That raised a question: How do you properly compensate an employee for a smash-hit,[9] million-dollar idea? On the one hand, you could argue that you don't have to—a software business is basically an idea factory. We were already paying Noah for his ideas. That was the nature of his employment agreement with us. Why pay twice?

But I felt we needed to do something else to express our gratitude. Should we buy Noah

---

[1] **bottom line** – profit or loss
[2] **spare time** – free time
[3] **self-absorbed drivel** – silly talk, nonsense that is focused on the person saying it or writing it
[4] **well-known** – familiar, recognized, widely known
[5] **little gears were turning in my head** – expression that means to think about something
[6] **code** – a system of signs or symbols that makes the structure and content for a website
[7] **polishing** – improving, refining
[8] **debugging** – finding and removing errors from something
[9] **smash-hit** – something that is very successful

an Xbox 360? Pay him a cash bonus? Maybe present him with a certificate of merit,[10] nicely laser-printed on heavyweight bond paper? Or a T-shirt that said "I Invented a Million-Dollar Business and All I Got Was This Lousy T-shirt"? We were stumped.[11]

And what about everybody else at Fog Creek? Those people were doing their jobs, too. Simply because one programmer's idea translated visibly and directly into a lot of money didn't mean that the other team members weren't adding just as much value to the business, albeit in a less direct way. At around the same time Noah came up with the classified ads idea, most of my employees were hard at work developing FogBugz 6.0, a smash hit that just about doubled our monthly sales.

Noah's case was only the most dramatic example of a question that has long intrigued me: How do you pay employees based on performance when performance is so hard to quantify? The very idea that you can rate knowledge workers on their productivity is highly suspect and always problematic. If you mess up, the consequences are very real.

Psychologists talk about two kinds of motivation: intrinsic and extrinsic. Intrinsic motivation is what drives you to do something regardless of whether you will receive a reward. Why do you spend an hour cleaning the inside of your stove? Nobody looks in there. Your intrinsic motivation compels you to do a thorough job. We all have it—in fact, most people start out with the desire to excel at whatever they do. Extrinsic motivation is the drive to do something precisely because you expect to receive compensation, and it's the weaker of the two.

The interesting thing, according to psychologists, is that extrinsic motivation has a way of displacing intrinsic motivation. The very act of rewarding workers for a job well done tends to make them think they are doing it solely for the reward; if the reward stops, the good work stops. And if the reward is too low, workers might think, Gosh, this is not worth it. They will forget their innate, intrinsic desire to do good work.

Plus, the minute you start giving bonuses to reward performance, people start to compare themselves with their coworkers. Why didn't I get as much?

And the grumblers have a point: It's impossible to know whether that bug[12] that David fixed on Tuesday made more or less money for Fog Creek than the code Ted added on Wednesday. We are not a piecework sweatshop[13] sewing doggie coats, where David made five and Ted made seven, so Ted should obviously get 40 percent more money.

In an environment in which judging performance is a subjective exercise, you are bound to make decisions with which employees disagree. Human beings, by their nature, tend to think of themselves as, how can I put this politely, a bit more wonderful than they really are. All of your B performers think they are A performers. The C performers think they are B performers. (A couple of your A performers think they are F performers, because they are crazy perfectionists or just clinically depressed. But they are the exceptions.)

So even if you did magically have the ability to accurately measure how good someone was at a job, the average worker, with his or her above-average opinion of his or her work, would still feel undervalued.

Throughout my career, I have observed that companies with formal systems that tie cash bonuses to performance end up with far more than half of their staff sulking[14] and unhappy. Back when I worked at Microsoft, one of my friends got a lousy review that was neither fair nor correct: His bosses rated him based on the 5 percent of the job they observed (his infrequent interactions with them) instead of the 95 percent of his job where he was exemplary (his frequent interactions with customers). Based on that review, he almost quit in despair[15] But he held on, and now he is a very senior executive in charge of a product so important that you, personally, will almost certainly use it today.

So, back to Noah, the guy with the million-dollar idea. Though we don't believe in performance bonuses, we still wanted to

[10] **certificate of merit** – an award for doing something well

[11] **stumped** – confused

[12] **bug** – programming error

[13] **piecework sweatshop** – reference to a factory where things are put together piece by piece

[14] **sulking** – being silent and angry

[15] **despair** – feeling of hopelessness

recognize his contribution. We decided to give Noah 10,000 shares of stock—conditional on him coming back to work for us full time when he graduated. Because Fog Creek is private and our stock is hard to value,[16] we could say "it's only fair that you share in the wealth" without assigning an actual dollar amount to it. It wasn't the perfect solution, but everybody thought it made sense.

Noah seemed pleased, and we hoped the stock would entice him to come back to Fog Creek to take a full-time job. Which . . . he didn't. Google made him a better offer. That's another flaw[17] with performance-based rewards: They are easy for one of your competitors to top.[18]

Oh, well. Thanks for the summer, Noah. We are keeping an empty office here in case you change your mind.

To read Joel Spolsky's column, go to www.inc.com/magazine/columns/howharditcoulditbe.

---

[16] **value** – estimate something or someone's worth

[17] **flaw** – fault, detracting feature
[18] **top** – do something better than someone else

▶ SKIMMING FOR DETAILS

F **Each statement below is false. Rewrite it to make it true.**

EXAMPLE: Joel Spolsky works as a programmer for Noah Weiss.

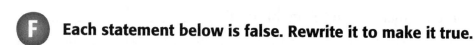
Noah Weiss works as a programmer for Joel Spolsky.

1. Noah suggested putting classified ads selling computers on Joel's blog.

   _____

2. At first, Joel loved the idea of putting ads on his blog.

   _____

3. 37signals gets 250 ads per month.

   _____

4. 37signals charges $350 per ad.

   _____

5. 37signals is a well-known software company in New York City.

   _____

6. Fog Creek decided to charge $250 for its ads.

   _____

7. The ad project made Fog Creek $2 million.

   _____

8. Joel used to work for Google.

_____

9. Fog Creek gave Noah a cash bonus for his great idea.

_____

10. Noah took a full-time job with Fog Creek.

_____

► MAIN IDEAS

G **Answer the questions.**

1. What idea did Noah come up with? _____

_____

2. How would the company make money from his idea? _____

_____

3. Why was Joel concerned with rewarding Noah for his great idea? _____

_____

4. What is the difference between intrinsic and extrinsic motivation? _____

_____

_____

5. What happened to Joel's friend at Microsoft? _____

_____

_____

6. How is the story related to Joel's problem of how to reward Noah? _____

_____

_____

7. How did Fog Creek decide to reward Noah? _____

_____

8. Do you think it was a good reward? Why or why not? _____

_____

► SUMMARIZE

H **Summarize the article using the suggestions below.**

1. What is the main idea of the article? (topic sentence) _____

   _____

2. What are some important facts from the article?

   a. _____

   b. _____

   c. _____

3. Briefly describe the problem Joel had.

   _____

   _____

   _____

4. What was the solution?

   _____

   _____

I **Write your summary below.**

_____

_____

_____

_____

_____

_____

_____

_____

_____

_____

_____

A A business letter is used to make requests, make complaints, give information, or make a recommendation. Read the letter that Noah Weiss wrote to his boss.

Noah Weiss
5654 85th Street
New York, NY 10006
November 5, 2009

Mr. Joel Spolsky
Fog Creek Software
55 Broadway, 25th Floor
New York, NY 10006

Dear Mr. Spolsky,

I know I have only been working at your company for a few months, but I have a great idea that I think will improve your bottom line. I think you should start posting ads for job listings on your blog. I think this will make you money for a variety of reasons. First of all, your blog is read by thousands of programmers each month, programmers who are always looking for new job opportunities. And, if you started posting these ads, even more programmers would flock to your site. Second, because so many programmers will be logging onto your site daily, advertisers will want to post their job listings there. And furthermore, because of all this traffic, you will be able to charge a premium for ad space, probably at least $250 per ad. The higher the price you put on your ads, the more valuable advertisers will think the space is. I believe this idea will make you a lot of money.

If you would like to talk about this idea some more, please don't hesitate to set up a meeting with me.

Thank you for your time,

Noah Weiss

Noah Weiss
Programmer

B Answer the questions about Noah's letter.

1. What is the purpose of Noah's letter?
2. What reasons does he give for why his idea is a good one?
3. If you were the owner of this company, would you set up a meeting to talk to Noah about his idea? Why or why not?

▶ CHOOSE A TOPIC

C **You will be writing a business letter that makes a suggestion or recommendation. Choose a topic below and circle it.**

1. Think of a way your classroom could be improved. Write a letter to your teacher.
2. Think of a way your school could be improved. Write a letter to your principal or dean.
3. Think of a way the company you work for could be improved. Write a letter to your supervisor or boss.
4. Think of a way a store you shop at or a company who provides a service to you could be improved. Write a letter to the company.

▶ BRAINSTORM

D **Based on the topic you chose, answer the following questions.**

1. What would you like to improve? _____

_____

2. What is your suggestion? _____

_____

_____

3. Why do you think this is a good idea?

   a. _____

   b. _____

   c. _____

   d. _____

E **Find the address of the person or company you will be addressing your letter to. Write it below.**

Name or Title of Person   _____

Name of Company   _____

Street Address   _____

_____

F How will you greet the person you are writing to? (*Note:* If you don't know the name of the person you are writing to, you can address your letter "To Whom it may Concern.")

_____

G How will you introduce yourself to the person reading your letter? How will you introduce your topic? Write your topic sentence below.

_____

_____

H How will you conclude your letter? Write your conclusion sentence below. (Remember to include a way to contact you if the person you are writing to doesn't know who you are.)

_____

_____

I Look back at the new words/expressions you learned in this unit from the vocabulary pages and from the Academic Word List. What words/expressions can you use in your business letter? Make a list of at least five below.

1. _____   4. _____

2. _____   5. _____

3. _____

▶ WRITE A ROUGH DRAFT

J Using all of the ideas you brainstormed, write your business letter on a separate piece of paper. Be sure to follow the format of the sample business letter on page 108. Start with your topic sentence. Make sure to use transitions to connect your main points. Do not forget to include some new vocabulary words!

▶ EDIT THE ROUGH DRAFT: Content

K Look back at your letter and answer the following questions.

1. Is my letter clearly written and easy to understand? _____

2. Did I explain who I was? _____

3. Did I explain why I was writing the letter? _____

4. Did I make a suggestion for improvement? _____

5. Did I include at least three reasons why I thought my suggestion was good? _____

6. Did I connect my ideas with transitions? _____

7. Did I include some of the new vocabulary words? _____ How many? _____

8. Did I conclude a way that the reader could contact me if necessary? _____

L   **Read your letter again and make any changes based on the questions you answered above.**

▶ EDIT THE ROUGH DRAFT: Format

M   **Answer the questions below to edit the *format* of your letter. Make sure you can say yes to every question.**

1. Are my name and return address in the top right hand corner?
2. Is the date below my address?
3. Are the name and address of the person/company I am writing to below my address, against the left margin?
4. Did I formally address the person I wrote to (Dear, To Whom it may Concern, etc.)?
5. Did I close my letter with *Sincerely?*
6. Did I print and sign my name?

▶ EDIT THE ROUGH DRAFT: Mechanics

N   **Use the editing checklist to edit the mechanics of your letter.**

✔ EDITING CHECKLIST

	Yes	No
The first letter of every sentence is capitalized.	☐	☐
Every sentence ends with a punctuation mark.	☐	☐
Every sentence has a subject and a verb.	☐	☐
The subject and the verb agree in every sentence.	☐	☐
All of the words are spelled correctly.	☐	☐
All of the words are in the correct order.	☐	☐

O   **Go back and make the formatting and mechanical changes to your letter.**

► PEER EDITING

P   Now, exchange your letter with a partner. Have your partner read your letter and answer the same questions to help you make formatting and mechanical changes.

Q   Have your partner answer the following questions about the content of your letter.

1. Is the letter clearly written and easy to understand? _____

2. Did the author explain who he/she was? _____

3. Did the author explain why he/she was writing the letter? _____

4. Did the author make a suggestion for improvement? _____

5. Did the author include at least three reasons why he/she thought the suggestion was good? _____

6. Did the author connect his/her ideas with transitions? _____

7. Did the author include some of the new vocabulary words? _____ How many? _____

8. Did the author conclude in a way that the reader could contact him/her if necessary? _____

R   Talk to your partner about your letter and go back and make any changes that you think will improve your story.

► WRITE THE FINAL LETTER

S   Write your final paper. Typing your letter on the computer will make it look professional.

T   Proof your final letter.

► Community Challenge

Mail your letter to the person you wrote it to and wait for a response. If the person responds, share the response with your class.

UNIT 8

Civic Responsibility

A There are many ways to get information about current events and issues in your local community, state, country, and the world. Some people watch television and some read the newspaper. Others get their news from the Internet. How do you get your news?

B There are times when you hear a news story or read an article that concerns you. You may think it is your civic duty to respond. How would you share your opinion with each of the following news sources?

News source	Way to share my opinion
newspaper	write a letter to the editor
news program on TV	
Internet news site	
radio program	

C If you were to share your opinion with a news source, what would be your reason for doing it? Rank each of the reasons below in order of importance to you (1 being the most important).

_____ inspire other people in my community to take action

_____ get my message out to political leaders and policy makers

_____ inspire a reporter to do more research on an issue

▶ VOCABULARY CHALLENGE

A **Look at the words. Check (✔) the words that you know.**

☐ accurate   ☐ amnesty   ☐ apathy   ☐ asylum   ☐ circumstances

☐ corrupt   ☐ detrimental   ☐ enforce   ☐ harbor   ☐ humanitarian

☐ perception   ☐ persecution   ☐ prohibit   ☐ unprecedented   ☐ validate

B **Read the paragraph below. Try to guess the meaning of each underlined word. Then, match the words to the correct definition.**

Immigrants come to this country seeking <u>asylum</u> under a variety of <u>circumstances</u>. Perhaps they were facing <u>persecution</u> in their own countries. Or maybe they want to escape a <u>corrupt</u> government. Although it is illegal to come to the United States undocumented, an <u>unprecedented</u> number of people cross the borders every day. Many are hoping for <u>amnesty</u>. The U.S. <u>prohibits</u> illegal immigration but has trouble <u>enforcing</u> the law. So the <u>perception</u> is that the U.S. <u>harbors</u> illegal immigrants. Do you think it is acceptable to illegally come into the U.S.?

_____ 1. asylum

_____ 2. circumstances

_____ 3. persecution

_____ 4. corrupt

_____ 5. unprecedented

_____ 6. amnesty

_____ 7. prohibit

_____ 8. enforce

_____ 9. perception

_____ 10. harbor

a. shelter or protect somebody
b. behaving in a way that is morally wrong
c. make sure a law or rule is obeyed
d. the conditions of your life
e. a pardon for doing something wrong
f. someone's way of thinking about something or something's impressions of a person
g. forbid or make illegal
h. allowing someone to stay usually because he or she is unable to return home safely
i. very great in quality or amount or something that has never happened before
j. being treated cruelly and unfairly

C Try to define each of the underlined words by reading the example sentence. Then, look up each word in a dictionary and see if you were correct.

1. They traveled to India for <u>humanitarian</u> reasons—to help rebuild homes that were destroyed in the earthquake.

   My definition: _____

   Dictionary definition: _____

2. Is it <u>accurate</u> to call people who illegally cross the border criminals, even if they are coming to avoid persecution in their own countries?

   My definition: _____

   Dictionary definition: _____

3. Can you <u>validate</u> that you really came here because you were being treated unfairly in your country?

   My definition: _____

   Dictionary definition: _____

4. It is <u>detrimental</u> to allow illegal immigrants to stay in our country because they take money away from our citizens.

   My definition: _____

   Dictionary definition: _____

5. Her <u>apathy</u> showed when she drove right by the people who had just been in an accident, even though they were flagging her down.

   My definition: _____

   Dictionary definition: _____

D Answer the questions.

1. Have you ever done anything for humanitarian reasons? If so, what? _____

   _____

2. Is it accurate to say that you are a citizen of this country? _____

   _____

3. How do people validate that they are allowed to drive a car in this country? _____

   _____

4. Do you do anything that could be considered detrimental to your health? (smoking, drinking, not exercising, etc.) _____

   _____

5. What are you apathetic about? _____

   _____

E Complete each sentence or question below with one of the words in the box. Each word will be used once.

accurate	amnesty	apathy	asylum	circumstances
corrupt	detrimental	enforcing	harbored	humanitarian
perception	persecution	prohibited	unprecedented	validate

1. Canada decided to close its borders to all immigrants and travelers, an

    _____ decision.

2. Many people came to the United States hoping that the president would grant them

    _____.

3. In order to be _____ by that immigrants' rights

    organization, you need to _____ that you arrived within
    the last month.

4. The first immigrants came to the United States from England because of

    religious _____.

5. It's not _____ to say that all illegal criminals are drug
    dealers.

6. Under what _____ did you move to this country?

7. It is now _____ for U.S. citizens to reenter the U.S. from
    Mexico without a valid birth certificate and driver's license, or a passport.

8. The border patrol agents have trouble _____ the law
    because there aren't enough of them.

9. Many people's _____ is that illegal immigrants don't pay
    taxes, which isn't true.

10. Do you think the government in our country is _____?

11. In a _____ effort, one group started collecting shoes to
    give to people whose shoes had been lost or worn out from crossing the borders.

12. It is _____ to put all illegal immigrants in the same
    category.

13. His _____ toward the people who swam across rivers to
    get here is surprising.

14. Because of the war going on in their country, the refugees were given

    _____ in the United States.

▶ ACADEMIC WORD LIST

F **Which words do you know?**

- ☐ amending
- ☐ challenges
- ☐ declined
- ☐ demonstrate
- ☐ depressed
- ☐ distinction
- ☐ eliminate
- ☐ estimated
- ☐ individuals
- ☐ labeled
- ☐ logic
- ☐ mechanism
- ☐ obtain
- ☐ promoted
- ☐ security
- ☐ seeking
- ☐ shifting
- ☐ temporary
- ☐ ultimately
- ☐ welfare

▶ DICTIONARY WORK: Review

Review what you learned about using a dictionary by completing the following exercises.

G **Find the parts of speech for the following words.**

1. depressed _____

2. distinction _____

3. decline _____

H **Write dictionary definitions for the following words.**

1. asylum: _____

_____

2. amnesty: _____

_____

3. persecution: _____

_____

4. welfare: _____

_____

I **Find example sentences in your dictionary for the following words.**

1. perception: _____

2. circumstances: _____

3. enforce: _____

J **Make vocabulary cards for the following words:** *apathy, harbor, detrimental*

► **PRE-READING**

A Why did you come to the United States? (If you still live in your native country, what would be your main reason for leaving?) Why do you think people permanently leave their native countries? Brainstorm your ideas below.

> **Reasons People Leave Their Native Countries**
>
> •
>
> •
>
> •
>
> •
>
> •
>
> •
>
> •
>
> •

B Some people come into the United States legally and others come illegally. Answer the following questions.

1. What is the process for legally coming to the United States from your country?

_____

_____

2. How do people illegally come to the United States?

_____

3. Do you think it is OK for people to come to the United States illegally? Why or why not?

_____

_____

4. Do you think it is OK for the United States to pay for benefits (education, medical benefits, etc.) for people who come to the United States illegally? Why or why not?

_____

_____

C An editorial is an article in a publication, such as a newspaper, that gives an opinion on a current issue or event. People usually write letters to respond to editorials. These letters are called Letters to the Editor. Read the editorial from *The American Times,* and then read the two opinion letters that follow.

The American Times

Opinion

EDITORIAL
Criminals or Refugees?
June 1, 2009

Did you know that there are thousands of people in Boulder, Colorado, who are breaking the law because they own a pet? That's right, owning a pet is illegal according to Colorado law. In Massachusetts, there is a law still on the books that prohibits using tomatoes in clam chowder. In Washington, it is illegal to go out in public with a cold. Who knows why these laws were passed, some as far back as 100 years ago. They are still on the books, but times changed, laws were not enforced, and they eventually lost their potency.[1] Laws are only as good as the public will to enforce them.

It has been reported that thousands of immigrants cross the U.S. border illegally every day. A few are drug peddlers[2] or criminals, but most are honest individuals or families seeking safe places to raise their children. Perhaps in the same way that we could claim a man fishing on a horse in Arizona is committing an illegal act according to laws on the books, we can also claim that immigrants crossing the border are illegal, but is it really accurate to call them criminals? Despite the concerns of some, the United States government has been relatively quiet on the subject and has promoted an open border through apathy. Even after terrorists from the Middle East successfully entered the United States and orchestrated[3] an attack on American soil in 2001, the president supported new legislation[4] to provide workers from other countries opportunities to work in the country on a temporary basis, a move that many believed to be a thinly veiled amnesty program. What is the message we send to the foreign born when people are routinely permitted to enter with little resistance and only token efforts are made to enforce the immigration laws? From the immigrants' point of view, the duplicity[5] of the existing and proposed immigration laws coupled with government inaction is an open invitation to enter.

Refugees are defined by international standards as people who have a fear of persecution because of race, religion, nationality, membership in a particular social group, or political opinion, and are accepted into another country as a place of safety. These fears are rooted[6] in the perception that their lives are in danger if they stay in their own country. There are thousands of asylum seekers who have arrived without papers to the United States and many have been allowed to stay for humane reasons. However, they did have to pass through formal hearings and were subject to scrutiny before they were permitted to stay. Obviously, many illegal immigrants cross the border undetected with less of a fear of death but legitimate concerns for their families' welfare due to economic strife and political abuses by their government. Because they don't fit into the international standard for refugees, there is no mechanism to process them. Nevertheless, these immigrants may very well consider themselves economic refugees with legitimate claims to human rights they don't receive in their home countries.

---

[1] **potency** – strength
[2] **drug peddlers** – people who sell drugs
[3] **orchestrated** – organized, coordinated
[4] **legislation** – a law or laws passed by a government
[5] **duplicity** – dishonesty, deceitfulness
[6] **rooted** – strongly related to

In 1986, the United States made an unprecedented move to offer amnesty to many undocumented immigrants. This action gave hope not only to the illegal aliens already in the country, but to others who saw a chance to move to a place of refuge and opportunities outside of their depressed and sometimes corrupt countries. Even if they didn't qualify for that round of amnesty, they hoped for another offer in the future. The plan included a tightening of the borders, but by and large, that part of the plan was not implemented with any sincere effort. Again, the United States legitimized illegal immigration and indirectly invited millions of economically challenged foreigners to seek new and better opportunities to raise their families.

There is no question that illegal immigration has put a strain[7] on the United States, particularly given the current economic downturn. Business owners who have relied on undocumented cheap labor often claim that they cannot find legal workers who are willing to take the jobs. But, with unemployment climbing over the 10 percent level, it is probable that more citizens are far more likely to take the jobs that they declined to do in the past, leaving immigrants out of work. I suspect many will claim that even with little work and difficult circumstances, they are still better off in the United States than where they came from. Growing tension between minorities labeled as undocumented or illegal will lead to more movements to declare that they should all be deported or treated as criminals. Perhaps we will see the majority of the public will[8] shifting, seeing these immigrants as less desirable and the enforcement of current law will change, but I hope that whatever challenges we face, humane solutions can prevail and the citizens of the United States can see these people as economic refugees who are not criminals, but honest people who were born in a country, by no fault of their own, where the blessings we enjoy don't exist.

Simon Demott

Letters to the Editor

While the *The American Times* is right in recognizing that illegal immigration is a problem for our country, Mr. Demott, in mentioning employment as the only issue, doesn't present the full magnitude[9] of the problem. First of all, millions of illegal aliens receive the benefits of free public education. Billions of taxpayer dollars are funneled[10] to this cause every year. In fact, federal law is clear that no public school can prohibit illegal aliens from an education. Furthermore, the citizen children of illegal immigrants can receive welfare benefits. The Legislative Analyst's Office declares that in California alone, over $500 million is expended on welfare for families of illegal aliens when one or more children is a citizen. 190,000 public school children are estimated to get benefits through their parents. What's more, the cost to house illegal aliens in prisons for violent crimes is staggering, not to mention the cost to society for their offenses. George Skelton wrote a column in 2008 saying that California spends $970 million on inmates[11] annually. Obviously the financial burden to the country amounts to several billion dollars and not merely a few jobs Americans won't do, as Mr. Demott seems to claim.

Mr. Demott tries, through logic, to make a distinction between illegal aliens as refugees or criminals. As noble as this idea appears, it doesn't change the fact that laws are being broken and consequences should be levied.[12] May I make a few observations? First, the very fact that the illegal aliens and their families are sneaking across the border in secret is in itself an admission that they are doing something wrong. It is naive[13] to believe that they are crossing the border secretly, but in reality the U.S. is "inviting" them here. Second, they need to work in order to survive here, so many of them obtain a social security number. Although I am sure many don't know where the numbers come from, they may be stolen. I echo Mr. Demott's slogan to treat immigrants humanely, but I don't believe that the solution should be in anyway validating illegal behavior. And yes, I believe Ronald Reagan was wrong in providing amnesty in 1986.

Judd Finchley, Tucson, AZ

[7] **strain** – make great demands on something
[8] **will** – determination, desire
[9] **magnitude** – importance
[10] **funneled** – resources concentrated somewhere
[11] **inmates** – people in prison
[12] **levied** – imposed, given
[13] **naive** – extremely simple and trusting

Bravo! Finally an article on undocumented immigrants that makes sense! I completely agree with Simon Demott and his editorial entitled "Criminals or Refugees." Immigrants come to our country because we have the best and most generous people in the world. To start, the people who go through the process to enter the country legally are generally more educated, more skilled, and have money. The government sees these legal immigrants as desirables because they demonstrate that they have ties to their native countries. This leaves the poor and misused people in second and third world countries without the option of entering with appropriate paperwork. They truly are economic refugees, as Mr. Demott coined[14] it. Maybe the international community should consider amending their definition. In addition, the U.S. offers humanitarian services throughout the world amounting to billions of dollars. The cost internally to help illegal immigrants certainly can't compare to what we give to foreign countries. Not only that, but when we give aid to governments, we often lose control of whether or not the money gets to those who really need it. I especially agree with Mr. Demott's plea[15] to treat these people humanely.

I am from Oklahoma where an experiment, in my view, has backfired drastically. In 2007, our state passed and implemented very strict[16] laws prohibiting employers from hiring illegal aliens and threatened that people would be arrested for harboring[17] the undocumented. As immigrants fled, businesses suffered. I even heard that the state Chamber of Commerce is trying to have the law repealed.[18] Apparently, this move has cost the state over a billion dollars. Cheap labor must be replaced with more costly workers, driving businesses to move out of the state. The business owners who are staying complain because they are required to operate as immigration police with no means to do it effectively. A problem I face on a regular basis is personal inconvenience. My family has lived here for 100 years. Nevertheless, because I look Hispanic, I have to carry my passport with me. On three occasions, I have been asked to prove my citizenship. Understand that I don't blame the fine people of Oklahoma. This is the result of laws that force us to look at people's skin color instead of their value to our communities. I fear that an approach to quickly eliminate illegal aliens from our country will ultimately be detrimental to our society.

Theresa Jones
Oklahoma City, OK

[14] **coined** – created an expression
[15] **plea** – urgent request

[16] **strict** – severe in maintaining discipline
[17] **harboring** – protecting
[18] **repealed** – undone, abolished

► READING COMPREHENSION

D **Circle the best answer.**

1. Simon Demott believes that most people crossing the border are _____.
   a. drug peddlers
   b. criminals
   c. honest individuals and families
   d. all of the above

2. What does Simon call a "thinly veiled amnesty program"?
   a. allowing immigrants to temporarily work in the U.S.
   b. granting amnesty to undocumented immigrants in 1986
   c. formal hearings for those seeking asylum
   d. all of the above

3. What are refugees?
   a. people afraid of persecution because of race
   b. people afraid of persecution because of religion
   c. people afraid of persecution because of nationality
   d. all of the above

4. Why did people want to come to the U.S. even if they didn't qualify for amnesty in 1986?
   a. The borders were tightened.
   b. They hoped amnesty would be offered again in the future.
   c. Millions of foreigners were invited to come to the United States.
   d. all of the above

5. What is NOT a reason illegal immigration has put a strain on the United States?
   a. Immigrants may be out of work as unemployment rises.
   b. Citizens may now be willing to take jobs that immigrants used to have.
   c. Immigrants are seen as undesirable.
   d. Unemployment has increased.

6. Judd Finchley _____ with Simon Demott.
   a. agrees
   b. disagrees

7. Theresa Jones _____ with Simon Demott.
   a. agrees
   b. disagrees

E **A fact is something that is true, something that can be proven. An opinion is an idea that someone believes, someone's personal point of view. Decide if each statement below is a fact or opinion. Write *fact* or *opinion* on the line.**

1. Amnesty was granted to many undocumented immigrants in 1986.

   _____

2. Citizens who are children of illegal immigrants can receive welfare benefits.

   _____

3. Immigrants come to our country because we have the best and most generous people in the world.

   _____

4. Immigrants consider themselves economic refugees with legitimate claims to human rights they don't receive in their home countries.

   _____

5. In Oklahoma in 2007, laws were passed that prohibited employers from hiring illegal immigrants.

   _____

6. People who go through the process to enter the country legally are generally more educated, more skilled, and have money.

   _____

7. Public schools cannot prohibit illegal aliens from getting an education.

   _____

8. The United States was attacked by terrorists in 2001.

   _____

9. An approach to quickly eliminate illegal aliens from our country would be detrimental to our society.

   _____

10. The United States government has promoted an open border through apathy.

   _____

F **Discuss your decisions with a classmate. Talk about what makes each statement a fact or an opinion. In some cases you may disagree.**

► OPINION SUPPORT

G **Judd Finchley believes that illegal immigration is putting a huge strain on the resources of the U.S. Government. What are the three main reasons he gives?**

1. _____

   _____

2. _____

   _____

3. _____

   _____

He also believes that immigrants who come here illegally are breaking the law and know they are breaking the law. What two examples does he give for this?

4. _____

   _____

5. _____

   _____

H **Theresa Jones agrees with Simon Demott's editorial. List at least four reasons she gives for believing that illegal immigration is not so bad.**

1. _____

   _____

2. _____

   _____

3. _____

   _____

4. _____

   _____

▶ WRITING CHALLENGE: Letter to the Editor

A Writing a letter to an editor of a magazine or newspaper is an effective way of sharing your opinion and possibly inspiring other people to take action on a particular issue. Think about the editorial and letters you read. Did they make you think about immigration differently? Were you able to see someone else's opinion on an important issue?

B Whenever you give your opinion on an issue, it is always a good idea to understand the other side of the issue. Sometimes it might even make you change your mind. Look at the opinion below.

> Students who are found to be illegal aliens should be deported back to their countries.

Do you agree or disagree with this opinion. Why or why not? Work with a partner or small group and brainstorm some ideas below. Come up with ideas supporting this opinion and against this opinion.

We agree because . . .

1. _____

2. _____

3. _____

We disagree because . . .

1. _____

2. _____

3. _____

C Look at each of the following statements. Decide if you agree or disagree with the opinion given in the statement. Write *agree* or *disagree* on the line.

1. It should be a school requirement for children and teenagers to exercise at least

   45 minutes per day. _____

2. All drugs should be legalized. _____

3. English should be the only language permitted in the United States. _____

► CHOOSE A TOPIC

D **Choose one topic from the previous page that seems the most interesting to you.**

E **Now, look at a sample brainstorm. Did you have any of the same ideas?**

> Students who are found to be illegal aliens should be deported back to their countries.

We agree because . . .

1. _Taxpayer dollars are paying for many of these students to go to school for free._

2. _If we allow them to stay here, we are saying it is OK to break the law._

3. _Most immigrants who come here to work send all the money they make back to their countries._

We disagree because . . .

1. _These students are trying to learn English so they can become productive members of society._

2. _These students will become educated and be valuable employees to American companies._

3. _These students will help teach their children English and make sure their children are better educated._

► BRAINSTORM

F **Write the topic you chose. Then, brainstorm ways in which you agree and disagree.**

TOPIC: _____

I agree because . . .

1. _____

_____

2. _____

_____

3. _____

_____

I disagree because . . .

1. _____

_____

2. _____

_____

3. _____

_____

G **Read the letter.**

> I disagree with your paper's point of view about illegal alien students being allowed to stay here and learn English. I think if these students are caught, they should be sent back to their countries. First of all, my tax dollars are helping pay for the free education many of these immigrants receive. This is taking money away from adult citizens who want to get an education. Furthermore, by allowing them to stay here, we are basically saying we have an open door policy and that anyone can come here illegally and stay. What's the point of having immigration laws if we don't enforce them? Finally, many of these students also have jobs and most of the money they make is sent back to their countries. How does this help our economy? I think by sending these students back to their native countries, we'll be sending a strong message to other immigrants who might try to come here illegally.
>
> Erika Mora
> Miami, FL

H **Write a letter for the other side of this issue. This is practice for your final writing. Focus on getting your ideas written down.**

▶ **WRITE A ROUGH DRAFT**

I **Using all of the ideas you brainstormed, write your letter on a separate piece of paper. It can be one paragraph, like the sample above, or two paragraphs like the letters you read on pages 120–121.**

1. Begin your letter with a topic sentence that clearly states your opinion.
2. Support your opinion with at least three ideas. Explain each idea more in depth if necessary.
3. Conclude by restating your opinion.

▶ EDIT THE ROUGH DRAFT

J Use the checklists below to edit the content and mechanics of your letter. When you are finished, ask a partner to read your letter and use the same checklists.

✔ EDITING CHECKLIST

	Me		My Partner	
Content	YES	NO	YES	NO
The letter is clearly written and easy to understand.	☐	☐	☐	☐
The letter clearly states an opinion.	☐	☐	☐	☐
The letter includes at least three reasons to support the opinion.	☐	☐	☐	☐
The ideas are connected with transitions.	☐	☐	☐	☐

✔ EDITING CHECKLIST

	Me		My Partner	
Mechanics	YES	NO	YES	NO
The first letter of every sentence is capitalized.	☐	☐	☐	☐
Every sentence ends with a punctuation mark.	☐	☐	☐	☐
Every sentence has a subject and a verb.	☐	☐	☐	☐
The subject and the verb agree in every sentence.	☐	☐	☐	☐
All of the words are spelled correctly.	☐	☐	☐	☐
All of the words are in the correct order.	☐	☐	☐	☐

K Read your letter again and make any changes based on the answers to the checklists.

▶ WRITE THE FINAL LETTER

L Write your final letter.

M Proof your final letter.

▶ Community Challenge

Write a letter to an editor of your school or local newspaper on an issue that you are passionate about. Be sure to check if your letter gets published in the newspaper.

▶ APPENDIX

▶ THE WRITING PROCESS

1 **Choose a topic**

Think about what you would like to write about. If you are in a class, your teacher will assign you a topic or give you topics to choose from. Also think about what type of writing you would like to write.

2 **Brainstorm**

After you have selected your topic, think about specific details you'd like to include in your writing. Using a chart like the ones below will help you organize your ideas.

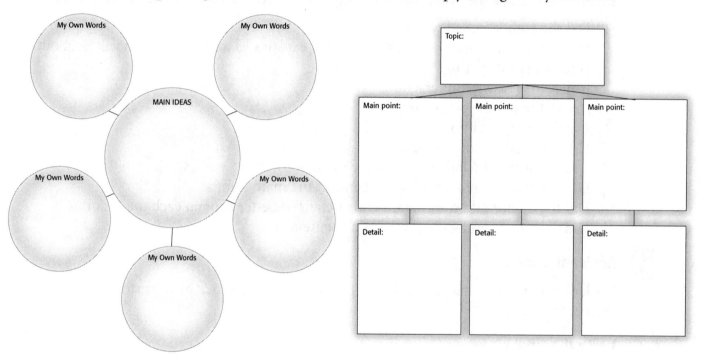

3 **Write a rough draft**

Using all of the ideas you have gathered, write your story on a separate piece of paper. Every time you begin a new idea or part of your story, start a new paragraph. Don't worry about your grammar or spelling—just concentrate on getting all your ideas down.

4 **Edit the rough draft**

Look over your rough draft and ask yourself these questions:

1. Is my story interesting?
2. Would someone be interested in reading my story?
3. Is my story easy to understand?
4. Did I include all the events, details, and thoughts from my brainstorming?
5. How could I make my story better?

Now that you've edited the content of your story, edit the mechanics. Mechanics are the spelling, grammar, and punctuation. Go through your story and ask yourself these questions:

1. Is every word of my title capitalized (except for small words)?
2. Is the first letter of every sentence capitalized?
3. Does every sentence end with a punctuation mark?
4. Does every sentence have a subject and a verb?
5. Do the subject and the verb agree in every sentence?
6. Are all of the words spelled correctly?

5 Peer edit

Exchange your story with a partner. Have your partner read your story and underline anything that he or she thinks needs editing. Your partner should answer these questions:

1. Did the author include a title?
2. Did the author include a topic sentence that explains what the paragraph will be about?
3. Is the story interesting?
4. Is the story easy to understand?
5. Are all the words spelled correctly?
6. Are there any grammar problems?
7. How could this story be better?
8. Did the author include at least three main points?
9. Did the author use transitions to connect the main points?
10. Did the author add some supporting details to better explain each main point?
11. Did the author end with a conclusion sentence?

6 Revise the draft

Look over the errors that you and your partner found. Go back to your story and correct these errors.

7 Write the final paper

Write your final paper. Remember the following formatting tips as you write:

1. Put the title at the top, center of your paper.
2. Put a space between the title and the first paragraph.
3. Indent the first word of every paragraph.
4. Make sure there are left and right margins on your paper.
5. Write neatly.

Instead of writing your final paper by hand, you may want to type it on the computer. This will make the final version of your paper look very nice and professional. And, it will make it easier to fix when you are proofing the final version.

8 Proof the final paper

Read your final paper and look for errors one more time. If you find any errors, go back and fix them.

► EDITING MARKS

Use these editing marks when reviewing your rough draft and your final paper. These marks will help you clearly identify what the errors are.

Symbol	Meaning	Example
∧	insert a word or words	I want to become ∧ drummer. *(a)*
⌐⌐	word order	Erin's phone |out|fell| of her pocket.
??	unclear meaning	She didn't want to not know. ??
#	error with number	Michael is one of the best swimmer here. #
℮	delete	The bicycle is is red.
→	indent paragraph	→ The city lights looked so beautiful that night.
VT	wrong verb tense	Yesterday Bill goes home. VT
WF	wrong word form	He is peeled the potatoes right now. WF
S/V	subject-verb agreement	The cows was grazing on the hill. S/V
ART	article error	I didn't eat ∧ cupcake. ART
≡	capitalize	The streets of boston are so confusing! ≡
/	lowercase	The computer is Not on.
FRAG	sentence fragment	Along the path. FRAG
CS	comma splice	They arrived early this morning, they won't make it to the party. CS
PRO	pronoun error	Nancy wore her pink dress last night. Everyone loved how he looked in it. PRO
REF?	unclear reference	Many grocery stores are beginning to carry locally grown foods. They are becoming more popular. REF?
RO	run-on	Sometimes people think that New York City is the capital of New York, but it isn't because Albany is and Albany isn't as popular. RO
⊙	insert period	The sky is full of clouds ⊙

► VOCABULARY LIST

*Academic Word List

Unit 1
community*
consisted*
coordinator*
couple*
courage
create*
despite*
discomfort
embark
energy*
equipment*
expertise*
found*
fulfilling
generate*
goal*
grade*
intriguing
instruct*
journal*
license*
mainstream
manifest
meditate
purchasing*
resign
role*
vibrant
vision*
visualize
visualizing*

Unit 2
accumulation
achieve*
affects*
alterations
aspects*
avoid
coincidence

contribute*
define*
devoted
dramatically*
economy*
enables*
enormous*
essence
establish*
forecast
fund*
identifying*
income*
invest*
maximize*
phase*
precisely
formulate
ongoing*
potential
retire
rewarding
revise*
risk
series*
significantly
speculate
strategy*

Unit 3
abrupt
adaptive*
adjusting*
advance
approaching*
capability*
constantly*
creating*
demonstration*
designed*
detects

dictate
display*
distraction
eliminating
enable
image*
impact*
industry
initial*
innovative
input*
maintain*
maximize
minor*
panic
potential*
proximity
restraints*
require*
selective
stability*
strides
trend
ultimately*

Unit 4
amenities
apparently*
approximately*
assimilated
boasts
civilization
community*
commutes
constant*
deemed
definitely*
diverse*
entities
environment*
equipped

facilitates*
features*
income*
innovation
issues*
location*
nevertheless*
obvious*
overall*
priorities
publication*
range*
reside
residents*
resources
requires*
shack
sufficient*
supply
tradeoffs

Unit 5
approach*
available*
benefit*
compensate
comprehensive
consists*
contracts*
expenditures
financial*
identity*
incentive
individuals*
deductible
mandate
medical*
obtained
option*
percent*
policy*

premiums
preventative
principle*
probability
procedures*
range*
reductions
referrals
reimbursement
requirements
restrictions
specific*
structure*
surgical
thereby*
variation*

Unit 6
accessibility
accountability
advocates
awareness
commitment*
commodity*
considerable*
consists*
consult
conventionally
convince*
corporate*
culture*
decline

derives
destruction
evidence
expand
global
gradual
implement
institute*
issues*
legitimate
logical*
policy*
preserve
relying*
researcher*
source
sustenance*
theory*
traditions*
transport*
version*

Unit 7
accurately*
assigning*
bond*
compels
compensate
community*
consequences*
consumers*
contribution

depressed*
desire
displacing*
draft*
dramatic*
entice
environment*
establish*
excel
exemplary
interactions*
intrigued
motivation
obviously*
precisely*
project*
psychologists*
publish*
resisted
revenue
reward
site*
solely*
subjective
thorough
visibly

Unit 8
accurate
amending*
amnesty
apathy

asylum
challenges*
circumstances
corrupt
declined*
demonstrate*
depressed*
detrimental
distinction*
eliminate*
enforce
estimated*
harbor
humanitarian
individuals*
labeled*
logic*
mechanism*
obtain*
perception
persecution
prohibit
promoted*
security*
seeking*
shifting*
temporary*
ultimately*
unprecedented
validate
welfare*

► IRREGULAR VERB FORMS

Base form	Simple past	Past participle	Base form	Simple past	Past participle
be	was, were	been	lose	lost	lost
become	became	became	make	made	made
begin	began	begun	mean	meant	meant
break	broke	broken	meet	met	met
bring	brought	brought	pay	paid	paid
build	built	built	put	put	put
buy	bought	bought	read	read	read
catch	caught	caught	ride	rode	ridden
come	came	come	run	ran	run
cost	cost	cost	say	said	said
do	did	done	sell	sold	sold
drink	drank	drunk	send	sent	sent
drive	drove	driven	set	set	set
eat	ate	eaten	show	showed	shown
fall	fell	fallen	sit	sat	sat
feel	felt	felt	sleep	slept	slept
fight	fought	fought	speak	spoke	spoken
find	found	found	spend	spent	spent
fly	flew	flown	spread	spread	spread
get	got	gotten	stand	stood	stood
give	gave	given	steal	stole	stolen
go	went	gone	take	took	taken
grow	grew	grown	teach	taught	taught
have	had	had	tell	told	told
hold	held	held	think	thought	thought
hurt	hurt	hurt	throw	threw	thrown
keep	kept	kept	wake	woke	woken
know	knew	known	wear	wore	worn
learn	learned	learned/learnt	win	won	won
lend	lent	lent	write	wrote	written

► CONJUGATED VERB LIST

Regular verbs

Base: work   **Infinitive:** to work

Simple present	**Present continuous**	**Simple past**	**Future**
I work	I am working	I worked	I will work
You work	You are working	You worked	You will work
We work	We are working	We worked	We will work
They work	They are working	They worked	They will work
He works	He is working	He worked	He will work
She works	She is working	She worked	She will work
It works	It is working	It worked	It will work

Past perfect	**Past continuous**	**Present perfect continuous**	**Past perfect**
I have worked	I was working	I have been working	I had worked
You have worked	You were working	You have been working	You had worked
We have worked	We were working	We have been working	We had worked
They have worked	They were working	They have been working	They had worked
He has worked	He was working	He has been working	He had worked
She has worked	She was working	She has been working	She had worked
It has worked	It was working	It has been working	It had worked

Base: study   **Infinitive:** to study

Simple present	**Present continuous**	**Simple past**	**Future**
I study	I am studying	I studied	I will study
You study	You are studying	You studied	You will study
We study	We are studying	We studied	We will study
They study	They are studying	They studied	They will study
He studies	He is studying	He studied	He will study
She studies	She is studying	She studied	She will study
It studies	It is studying	It studied	It will study

Past perfect	**Past continuous**	**Present perfect continuous**	**Past perfect**
I have studied	I was studying	I have been studying	I had studied
You have studied	You were studying	You have been studying	You had studied
We have studied	We were studying	We have been studying	We had studied
They have studied	They were studying	They have been studying	They had studied
He has studied	He was studying	He has been studying	He had studied
She has studied	She was studying	She has been studying	She had studied
It has studied	It was studying	It has been studying	It had studied

Irregular verbs

Base: have   **Infinitive:** to have

Simple present	Present continuous	Simple past	Future
I have	I am having	I had	I will have
You have	You are having	You had	You will have
We have	We are having	We had	We will have
They have	They are having	They had	They will have
He has	He is having	He had	He will have
She has	She is having	She had	She will have
It has	It is having	It had	It will have

Past perfect	Past continuous	Present perfect continuous	Past perfect
I have had	I was having	I have been having	I had had
You have had	You were having	You have been having	You had had
We have had	We were having	We have been having	We had had
They have had	They were having	They have been having	They had had
He has had	He was having	He has been having	He had had
She has had	She was having	She has been having	She had had
It has had	It was having	It has been having	It had had

Base: run   **Infinitive:** to run

Simple present	Present continuous	Simple past	Future
I run	I am running	I ran	I will run
You run	You are running	You ran	You will run
We run	We are running	We ran	We will run
They run	They are running	They ran	They will run
He runs	He is running	He ran	He will run
She runs	She is running	She ran	She will run
It runs	It is running	It ran	It will run

Past perfect	Past continuous	Present perfect continuous	Past perfect
I have run	I was running	I have been running	I had run
You have run	You were running	You have been running	You had run
We have run	We were running	We have been running	We had run
They have run	They were running	They have been running	They had run
He has run	He was running	He has been running	He had run
She has run	She was running	She has been running	She had run
It has run	It was running	It has been running	It had run